Cooking for One

By Nancy Creech

WINGS BOOKS

New York • Avenel, New Jersey

To my grandmother, Ruth Creech,
and to my sister, Louisa Creech

Previously titled *Cooking for Someone Special—Yourself*

Illustrations by Liz Hemingway
Book design by Andrea Gray
Copyright ©1985 by Storey Communications, Inc.

This 1995 edition is published by Wings Books, distributed by Random House Value Publishing, Inc., 40 Engelhard Avenue, Avenel, New Jersey 07001, by arrangement with Storey Communications, Inc.

Random House
New York • Toronto • London • Sydney • Auckland

Printed and bound in the United States of America

Library of Congress Cataloging-in-Publication Data
Creech, Nancy.
     [Cooking for someone special—yourself]
     Cooking for one / by Nancy Creech.
        p. cm.
     Originally published: Cooking for someone special—yourself.
  Pownal, Vt. : Storey Pub., 1985.
     Includes index.
     ISBN 0-517-14662-2
     1. Cookery for one.   I. Title.
  TX652.C777 1995
  641.5'61—dc20   95-9827
                                CIP

8 7 6 5 4 3 2 1

CONTENTS

iii

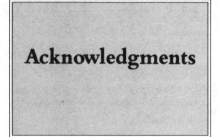

Acknowledgments

Foremost in my thoughts is gratitude to my family for their support and encouragement during this six-year project. Special thanks go to each of my parents, John Creech and Genevieve Creech, for their continuing expressions of confidence.

There are many whose donations of thought and labor were tangible and significant. Mary Jane Atkins provided the kind of rock-solid, day-to-day assistance I couldn't have done without. She would appear with groceries, provide typing paper, feed my cat, and, when it came to the finish, she pulled more than a few all-nighters at the typewriter. She didn't hesitate to provide editorial comment as well, and that proved enormously helpful.

The recipes were tested in many ways outside my own kitchen. Thanks go to Ron Albers, who cooked with me on countless Sundays and whose sense of adventure and confident technique were both inspiring and contributory. My five sisters, Kathleen Childs, Kristen Rowlen, Andrea Leichtfuss, Louisa Creech, and Rondi Creech, all did their share, as did my mother, Genevieve, and Anna Hazan, Adam Greenberg, Diana Kirchhoff, Gilbert Pilgram, and Richard Gilbert.

Sharon Jones painstakingly photocopied a lifetime collection of recipe clippings, and these proved to be a continuing source of information and inspiration which cannot be otherwise acknowledged.

Editorial assistance came from many quarters. Valuable pointers were received from my father, John, from his wife, Nancy Creech, and from Colin Alexander. Harriet Mullaney's many expressions of encouragement are deserving of special mention. Her excellent comments brought polish to my rough draft.

Production of the rough draft would not have gone as well as it did without the use of the sophisticated word processing equipment so generously made available to me by Alvin Pelavin.

Jill Mason of Garden Way Publishing did a truly fine job of combing through the highly detailed text, seeking clarification and correcting errors and inconsistencies. Her patience and meticulous attention to the many fine points in the text made the final editing phase go very smoothly.

Finally, my friend and mentor Pat LaGrave must be thanked as a constant source of inspiration. Her enthusiasm for food is truly infectious, and the substantive comments she contributed to my draft enhanced the text immeasurably.

Nancy Creech

INTRODUCTION

This cookbook is intended to be a resource for people cooking just for themselves who want to cook from scratch using commonly available ingredients. The editorial bias of the book is that people should cook and eat a variety of simple foods, and that single cooks could use some assistance in doing this. The person cooking for one deserves a resource cookbook complete enough to offer a range of small portion recipes when he or she chooses to cook.

There are 17.8 million Americans who officially occupy single-person households, according to the 1980 *U.S. Census*, an increase of 6.9 million since 1970. In addition to this large group there are millions more who share a kitchen with others, but who cook just for themselves: students living off campus, city dwellers sharing a flat, and people living with partners who have different schedules or dietary needs.

Such a significant segment of the population cannot be characterized as a group of rushed junk-food lovers in search of mates. The population of single people in America is as diverse as the population at large. If any generalization is appropriate, it is that single people are faced with many barriers to eating well regularly.

Shopping for one can be more difficult than cooking. Supermarkets often do not meet our needs with respect to packaging, so a single person must be an extraordinary manager to avoid wasting the often perishable excess food he or she must buy. It is therefore a goal of this book to provide answers and ideas on how some of the waste might be avoided.

Throughout this cookbook the user will discover again and again that cooking for one isn't different from "normal" cooking. There's no need for strange little sectional pots and pans, no need to memorize conversion tables. Most of the recipes in this book are quite flexible. Some are quick and easy, others are more elaborate; all use simple ingredients that are easy to find, and straightforward methods that will serve you regardless of the size of the portion.

Orientation

The quality of food available to all Americans has been a subject of controversy for the past two decades, particularly with respect to artificial ingredients in foods. When the recipes for this cookbook were developed, it was with this issue in mind. The ingredients you'll find here are plain foods, either raw, fresh, or packaged, available to most of us at the supermarket.

In doing research for this cookbook it was difficult not to be influenced by the "new vegetarians," that is, the vegetarians who embrace this diet for very compelling reasons no less ambitious than ending world hunger and re-ordering a truly unjust and unbalanced world economy. While I came to feel much compassion for these causes and the relationship of the human diet to them, I ultimately concluded that since I have not chosen this path as my own response, it would be false to reflect it in this cookbook. For several reasons, however, this cookbook does provide many alternatives to a red-meat-based diet and places greater emphasis on beans, grains, vegetables, chicken, and fish as sources of protein. Vegetarians will find ample main-dish recipes to meet their dietary requirements, in addition to an array of recipes for side dishes, salads, sauces, and desserts.

Methods

The recipes in this cookbook were either developed by me, adapted from recipes given to me, or, in the case of standard recipes such as yeast bread and soup stock, developed by me after conducting research in several text sources. All recipes and their variations were tested in my kitchen using a gas stove and conventional gas oven. Some recipes were also tested by friends. In my kitchen the cookware used was made of heavy aluminum alloy, heavy enamel, or cast iron because those materials conduct heat evenly and hold it well. If you are cooking with thin metal pans, they will get hot much faster, and cooking times may be somewhat shorter than indicated in the recipes in this book.

Herbs

The oft-stated rule is that twice the amount of fresh herbs as dried is needed to achieve the same result. This is true with some reservations. Dried herbs are subject to loss of flavor over time, and if your dried herbs are stale, you won't get the result desired. The flavors of fresh and dried herbs can be very different, and since fresh herbs are unavailable to most of us unless we cultivate them ourselves, the recipes in this cookbook assume the use of dried herbs unless otherwise specified.

Dried herbs should be crushed to increase their surface area, so that more flavor can be released and absorbed into the food. Crushing is preferable to grinding, which leaves a residue and some bitterness. Dried herbs such as basil, oregano, thyme, and marjoram are simply crushed between the fingers as they go into the pot. Celery seed can be crushed in a mortar and pestle. I keep one on the counter and use it often. If a mortar and pestle is unavailable, the back of a spoon will do. Other seeds can be crushed this way as well. Sage is actually "rubbed" to give it the proper texture. Ground sage is available, but is not preferred because it contains the rougher veins and stems which are eliminated through rubbing. Rubbed sage is fluffy and light in appearance, and that's the way it is usually sold.

Spices, such as roots and bark, are usually ground and can be purchased in that form.

I hope in using this cookbook that you will discover many ways to prepare and enjoy familiar and new foods. Cooking for one can be a daily adventure, accomplished at low cost, in little time, and with great pleasure.

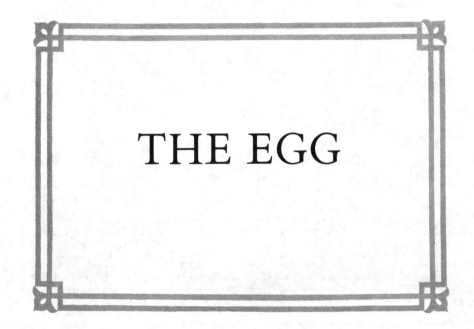

THE EGG

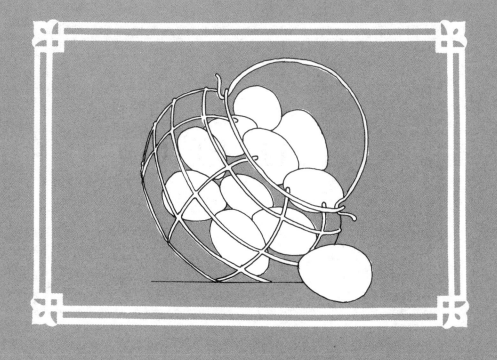

A dozen eggs is often too many for a single person to have on hand. Having so many eggs creates pressure to use them up. Whenever you can, buy a half-dozen eggs at a time. You can comfortably work these into your meals over a week-long period, eaten plain and used in cooking.

If your refrigerator has an egg shelf for individual storage of eggs, use it to store only hard-cooked eggs—eggs have porous shells and will dry out if placed there.

Omelet

To make any omelet, your pan should be "seasoned" to prevent sticking. Generously oil a clean pan (preferably an omelet pan, which has gently sloped sides) and place it on a burner with the flame on low to medium heat. Leave the pan on the heat for about 4 minutes. Turn off the heat and allow the pan to sit for 5–10 minutes. Then wipe away the oil with a paper towel, and the pan is seasoned.

1 teaspoon butter
1 egg
1½ tablespoons milk or water

Over medium heat melt the butter in the seasoned omelet pan.

In a bowl, beat the egg briefly with the liquid. Once the butter is melted and the pan is medium hot (and not before!), pour the egg into the omelet pan. It should begin cooking the moment it hits the pan.

With a spatula, very gently move the egg away from the sides of the pan and allow the egg to very gently flow to the bottom for cooking. Let the egg do the work itself —you don't want to do anything vigorous here. The omelet is cooked when all liquid stops flowing from the top of the egg. At this point, add any filling you have ready.

Fold the omelet in half. It should cooperate. Tip the pan and gently coax the upper half to flip over onto the lower half. Then slide the omelet onto your plate.

Variations

An omelet is a great way to use up leftovers such as steamed vegetables. Check what you have in the refrigerator for likely candidates. Heat the omelet filling before you start the egg because the egg takes only moments to cook. Here are a few fillings you may want to try:

- avocado slices (room temperature is warm enough)
- broccoli, green beans, or spinach (chopped, cooked, and drained)
- chunky tomato sauce
- grated red cabbage (gently steamed first)

Egg Benedict with Cheddar

I developed this recipe one Sunday morning when I was yearning for Eggs Benedict but had no Canadian bacon on hand. Cheddar is a marvelous substitute! Its natural pungence and saltiness make it a good, rich companion to the Hollandaise Sauce.

Make the sauce before you poach the egg. It can be kept warm in a hot water bath.

½ **Hollandaise Sauce recipe (p. 178)**
1 **thick slice bread, or English muffin half**
1 **thick slice cheddar cheese**
1 **egg**

Preheat the oven to 200° F.

Toast and butter the bread and top it with the cheddar. Place this in the oven to warm while you poach the egg.

Add about 1½ inches of water to a skillet, bring it to a simmer, and break the egg into it. When the egg is poached (in about 3 minutes), remove the toast and cheese from the oven and use a slotted spoon to place the egg on the cheese. Top with the warm Hollandaise Sauce and serve immediately.

Egg Florentine

The word "Florentine" in the title tells you that this dish is made with spinach. Use fresh leaves if possible— the difference between fresh and frozen here is distinct.

You'll want to make the Béchamel Sauce first. Keep it warm in a hot water bath on the back burner while you cook the spinach. This way the assembled dish will go into the oven already warm and will reduce cooking time.

½ **Béchamel Sauce recipe (p. 182)**
1 **teaspoon vegetable oil (if fresh spinach is being used)**
2–3 **large, fresh spinach leaves, washed and patted dry, or ¼ package of frozen spinach, cooked and drained**
1–2 **eggs**

Preheat the oven to 350° F.

Lightly oil an individual casserole dish and warm it in the oven.

If you are using fresh spinach, heat 1 teaspoon oil in a frying pan and add the spinach leaves to it.

Coat the leaves with the hot oil, then cover for 3 minutes over low heat.

If you are using frozen spinach, cut ¼ off a frozen 10-ounce brick and cook it in a small saucepan in ¼ inch boiling water. Drain.

Place the cooked spinach in the casserole dish and make indentations for 1 or 2 eggs. Break the eggs into the spinach and top with the warm Béchamel Sauce. Bake in the preheated oven for 15–20 minutes. Serve warm.

The baked egg is an excellent candidate for a one-dish meal when combined with any vegetable, cheese, or sauce. This recipe is just one example—others follow.

Olive oil is preferable here for the sake of authenticity, but you may substitute any vegetable oil except peanut oil and get good results.

1 teaspoon vegetable oil
1 garlic clove, minced
1 teaspoon chopped onion
1 teaspoon chopped green pepper
1–2 eggs
1 tablespoon grated Parmesan cheese, or breadcrumbs

Preheat the oven to 325° F.

Oil an individual casserole dish. Also add 1 teaspoon oil to a small frying pan. Sauté the garlic and chopped vegetables in the frying pan with the oil. Then place the sautéed vegetables in the bottom of the individual casserole dish.

Break the eggs over the vegetables. Top them with the Parmesan cheese or breadcrumbs. Bake for 15 minutes, or until the eggs are set but not hard. Serve at once.

❧ POACHED EGG COMPANIONS ❧

Toast is just one companion for a poached egg. Choose any one of the following as a nest:
- steamed broccoli or cauliflower florets
- steamed asparagus spears
- steamed grated carrots (done in moments!)
- steamed spinach (fresh or frozen)
- steamed rice flavored with curry
- steamed fresh green beans
- leftover spaghetti sauce, heated

Top with:
- a pat of butter, herbed or with lemon
- grated Parmesan cheese
- cream sauce in any of its infinite variations
- grated Swiss, cheddar, or Monterey Jack...
- a sprinkling of breadcrumbs

Basic One-Egg Soufflé

A soufflé is a marvel! It combines a thick sauce, which binds and flavors the dish, and a light and airy portion, which holds it up. The trick is to combine these two diverse parts and cook them in such a way that the egg whites hold their airiness.

1½ teaspoons butter
1½ teaspoons unbleached, all-purpose flour
¼ cup milk (preferably at room temperature)
1 egg, separated
pinch salt
pinch pepper
pinch cream of tartar

Preheat the oven to 400° F.

Generously butter an individual casserole dish with vertical sides, and chill it until baking time. Remove the upper rack in your oven.

Melt the butter in a small frying pan and add the flour to it. Let the mixture cook for a minute or so, then slowly add the milk while stirring quickly with a wire whisk. Let this bubble for about a minute. Turn off the burner and *then* add the egg yolk, stirring quickly. Next, stir in the salt and pepper and let this mixture cool until it is just warm. It mustn't be hot when the egg whites are folded in.

In a dry mixing bowl and using a dry wire whisk, combine the cream of tartar and the egg white. Beat the egg white to firm, shiny peaks. Don't let them get dry.

Immediately fold half the whites into the yolk mixture. Then fold in the second half. Turn the mixture into the chilled soufflé dish.

Place the soufflé in the oven and immediately reduce the heat to 350° F. Bake for 30 to 35 minutes. Don't open the oven door until the time is up!!

Upon removing the soufflé from the oven, serve immediately.

Mushroom Soufflé

The Mushroom Soufflé is a classic. Mushrooms and eggs are always a good combination.

2 teaspoons butter
3–4 medium-sized mushrooms, chopped fine
1½ teaspoons unbleached, all-purpose flour
¼ cup milk (preferably at room temperature)
1 egg, separated
2 teaspoons grated Parmesan cheese

Preheat the oven to 400° F.

Generously butter an individual casserole dish with vertical sides, and chill it until baking time. Remove the upper rack in your oven.

Melt the butter in a sauté pan. Add the chopped mushrooms and sauté until thoroughly heated. Add the flour and mix thoroughly. Allow to cook for about 30 seconds, then add the milk, stirring constantly, and permit this mixture to heat thoroughly. Cook for about a minute, then turn off the burner.

Stir the egg yolk into the mushroom mixture with a wire whisk. Allow this mixture to sit while you beat the egg white to peaks that are stiff but not dry. Gently fold half the egg white into the mushroom mixture, then add the second half, and complete folding.

Remove the chilled soufflé dish from the refrigerator and coat it with the grated Parmesan cheese, patting if necessary to make it stick. Turn the soufflé mixture into this dish and place it on the lower rack of your preheated oven. Reduce the heat to 350° F. and bake for 30–35 minutes. Serve immediately.

This is a great way to use up left-over cooked eggplant. Have the soufflé for dinner with a thick slice of wheat bread.

2 teaspoons finely chopped onion
2 teaspoons butter
1½ teaspoons unbleached, all-purpose flour
¼ cup milk (preferably at room temperature)
pinch turmeric
pinch cumin
pinch cayenne
pinch salt
2 tablespoons cooked and mashed eggplant
1 egg, separated

Preheat the oven to 400° F.

Generously butter an individual casserole dish with vertical sides, and chill it until baking time. Remove the upper rack of your oven.

Sauté the onion in the butter until the onion is translucent. Add the flour and mix thoroughly. Cook for about 30 seconds. Add the milk, stirring constantly with a wire whisk. Allow this mixture to cook for about a minute. While it is cooking, add the spices and salt. Then add the eggplant and heat thoroughly.

Turn off the burner and add the egg yolk. Stir it in vigorously with a wire whisk and then allow the mixture to sit.

Whip the egg white to peaks that are stiff but not dry. Fold half of this into the eggplant mixture. Then fold in the other half. Turn the mixture into the chilled soufflé dish and immediately place it in the preheated oven. Reduce the heat to 350° F. Bake for 30–35 minutes and serve immediately upon removing from the oven.

Variation

Season some extra eggplant and spread a layer on the bottom of the soufflé dish before adding the egg mixture.

Egg Baked in Tomato

This makes a tidy and comfortable breakfast—or lunch or dinner!

1 medium-sized tomato
pinch salt
pinch pepper
¼ teaspoon dill weed
2 teaspoons grated Parmesan
   cheese
1 egg

Preheat the oven to 350° F.

Begin preparation by oiling a small casserole dish (about 1½-cup capacity) and warming it in the oven.

Slice the top off the tomato and gently squeeze the pulp and juice into a bowl. Sprinkle salt, pepper, and dill weed into the tomato's interior.

Add the Parmesan cheese to the reserved tomato pulp. Divide this mixture in half. Place one half in the bottom of the hollowed-out tomato. Break the egg into the tomato shell and top with the other half of the pulp mixture.

Place the stuffed tomato in the casserole dish and bake in the oven for 20 minutes. Serve.

Broccoli Frittata

A frittata is a quiche without a crust—an egg custard cooked either on top of the stove or in the oven. For this recipe, the frittata will cook on top of the stove. Cold frittata makes an excellent alternative to a sandwich.

1 tablespoon vegetable oil
¼ broccoli bunch, cut into bite-
   sized pieces
1-1½ teaspoons soy sauce
⅓ cup water
½ teaspoon nutmeg
2 tablespoons butter
2 eggs, beaten
¼ cup milk

In a small skillet, add the oil and make sure it is *hot*; then add the broccoli and soy sauce. Stir for about a minute. Add the water and cover. Steam the vegetable for 6–7 minutes, then drain, keeping the broccoli in the skillet with the burner on low. Sprinkle the steamed broccoli with the nutmeg.

Add the butter and allow it to melt, coating the broccoli and the sides of the pan. Then combine the egg and milk. Add the egg mixture to the pan and cook over very low heat for about 6 minutes or until set. Don't stir. When done, you can use a spatula to lift or tip the whole frittata onto a plate for serving.

Curried Egg Stew

Here's an egg dish that can be featured at lunch or dinner. The eggs aren't really stewed—they're hard-cooked and then added to tomatoes simmered in a wonderful bouquet of Indian spices. Plan ahead by hard-cooking 2 eggs and steaming ¼ cup rice in ½ cup water or broth.

2 tablespoons butter
1 medium-sized onion, quartered
    and sliced thin
1 garlic clove, minced
1 medium-sized tomato, chopped
pinch salt
pinch turmeric
pinch ginger
½ teaspoon coriander
½ teaspoon cumin
½ teaspoon paprika
2 eggs, hard-cooked
½ teaspoon garam masala (p. 191),
    optional
½ cup cooked rice

Melt the butter in a medium-sized skillet. Then add the onion and garlic and cook until the onion is translucent. Add the tomato to the onion and sauté for a few minutes until the tomato steams.

As the tomato sautés, add the salt and spices (except the garam masala) and continue to cook for 30 minutes over very low heat, stirring occasionally. Halve the hard-cooked eggs and add them and the garam masala to the tomato mixture. Heat through and serve over the rice.

SOUPS

Making your own soup is one of the finest solitary activities I know. A few of these soups make more than one or two servings, but that shouldn't be a problem. If you have a cup or two left over, you'll discover the truth to the old cliché: it's better the second day! Of course, there are many ways to make single-serving soups; these recipes are only a sampling of what is possible.

Making stock is an important part of soup making, but it doesn't have to be made at the same time. Any freshly made broth or stock can be frozen once it has cooled and the hardened fat has been skimmed off. Fish and vegetable stocks should be used immediately once thawed.

Ham Stock

4 CUPS

Ham stock is a little different from other red meat stock. It is made in less time than beef stock and is often immediately incorporated into a bean soup.

Plan on a total cooking time of about 3 hours if you want to produce a tasty soup. Once the ham bone has been removed, add the ham dice, along with any vegetables or grains, and simmer for an additional hour. If you want to make the soup later, you can freeze the ham stock—once it's been brought to room temperature and strained. Milk cartons can be used to freeze ham stock in sensible quantities. ❧

1 ham bone
6 cups cold water
1 onion
3 whole cloves
1 carrot, scrubbed
1 celery rib
2 parsley sprigs
6 peppercorns, lightly crushed
1 bay leaf

Trim the meat and fat from the ham bone. Cover the bone with the cold water, and turn the burner to high.

Stick the onion with the cloves. Add the remaining ingredients to the ham bone and water. Bring to a boil, then reduce heat and simmer for 1½–2 hours. Remove the ham bone. Strain and discard any solid material.

Basic Beef Stock

This project will require your attention for the first hour and a half; then the stock can simmer on its own for 6 hours or so. To begin, you'll need a cookie sheet and a soup pot.

2 pounds soup bones (beef or veal bones)
½ large onion, cut in wedges
1 carrot, cut into 1-inch lengths
6 cups cold water
1 celery rib, cut into 1-inch lengths
4–6 peppercorns, lightly crushed
1 bay leaf
½ teaspoon salt

Preheat the oven to 425° F.

Arrange the soup bones and the onion and carrot pieces on a cookie sheet and place it in the hot oven. Rotate the pieces every 15 minutes and remove after 1 hour. The bones and vegetables should be dark brown.

Individually place the brown pieces, without the fat, in a soup pot and cover with the 6 cups *cold* water. This will permit the flavors to flow from the meat into the water. Add the remaining ingredients. Turn the burner onto high.

Pour off the fat from the cookie sheet and discard it. Place the cookie sheet on a burner over medium heat. Add 1 cup cold water and use the water and a spatula to scrape the caramelized pieces of meat and vegetable from the surface of the cookie sheet. This step is called deglazing. Add the now brown water to the soup pot along with any pieces of meat and vegetable scraped from the cookie sheet.

As the bones heat in the soup pot, a foam will form at the surface for the first half-hour or so. This "scum" should be skimmed from the surface. Once this skimming period is over, loosely cover the pot and reduce the heat to a quiet simmer. Simmer for 6 hours.

After 6 hours, strain the stock into a bowl and let it sit overnight in the refrigerator. All the fat will rise to the top and solidify. In the morning, remove and discard the fat.

If you intend to freeze any of the stock, do so in 1–2-cup portions for convenient future use. If you freeze in jars, leave at least 1 inch of space between the top of the stock and the lid of the jar to allow for swelling during freezing.

⇒BROTHS⇐

Packaged broths aren't as rich as stocks, but they make handy substitutes when no stock is available. Don't hesitate to take that shortcut! Bouillon cubes are another alternative, but one to be used with caution because they often contain additives, and they can become rancid.

Chicken Stock

You can make this stock in about an hour and a half, but allow additional time for it to chill in the refrigerator so you can skim off the fat.

chicken feet, wings, neck, and back, chopped in one or two places
2 tablespoons vegetable oil
2 quarts cold water
chicken organs
1 onion, including skin, cut in wedges
4 celery ribs, sliced
4–5 peppercorns
1 bay leaf
¼ teaspoon salt, optional

In the bottom of a soup pot, brown the chicken pieces in hot oil. Pour the cold water over the browned chicken. Add the chicken organs, onion, celery, peppercorns, and bay leaf and bring to a boil. Boil for about 2 minutes, then reduce the heat to a simmer. Cook for 45 minutes, skimming the residue or scum from the top of the soup as it collects. Taste! Then, if desired, add the salt once the stock has almost finished simmering.

Once the broth has cooled, skim off the fat that has risen to the top. Then, if you don't plan to use it soon, freeze the broth in 1-cup containers or in ice cube trays (transferring the cubes to a plastic bag once frozen).

Fish Stock

This is the easiest stock of all to make. It is usually made as a companion to a fish dish such as oyster stew or clam chowder.

2 cups cold water
1 cup available fish or shellfish trimmings, such as heads, fins, tails, or bones
1 bay leaf
1 onion, cut in quarters
1 celery rib
3–4 peppercorns

Combine all the ingredients in a large pot, and bring the mixture to a boil. Then simmer for 15–20 minutes *at the most.* Skim while cooking and, if a clear stock is desired, strain when finished.

Variations

Try adding one or more of the following to the simmering stock: peppercorns, lemon rind, bouquet garni (p. 189), wine, vermouth, or vinegar.

Vegetable Stock

While making a vegetable stock is a marvelous way to purge your crisper, it is necessary to be somewhat discriminating in your choice of ingredients for the stock. I would pass over very old, very limp greens because of the bitterness they may impart. Generally, complement your older vegetables with plenty of fresh, ripe vegetables in season.

The rule of thumb is to use equal amounts of vegetables and cold water. You may want to increase the water. Chop the vegetables in their skins into ¾-inch cubes.

**¾ cup chopped broccoli stems
and florets**
⅓ cup diced carrot
⅓ cup diced celery
1½ cups cold water
2 teaspoons fresh parsley, chopped
⅛ teaspoon celery seed
⅛ teaspoon salt, optional

Place all the ingredients in a blender and process until smooth.

In a saucepan over medium heat, bring the stock almost to a boil; then reduce the heat and simmer for 15 minutes. (The vitamins in the vegetables will be destroyed with prolonged cooking.) Taste for flavor and correct the seasoning, if desired, with soy sauce, Worcestershire sauce, or salt and pepper. You'll want it to taste good before you use it in anything else! Do let your palate discover the vegetable flavors, though—don't mask them, thinking salty is the only kind of broth.

Strain the broth or leave it as is and store it in the refrigerator. Use it within three days.

Mushroom and Barley Soup

This is a very thick soup—almost a stew. When preparing the vegetables, slice them all to a thickness of about ¼ inch.

¼ cup whole, hulled barley, washed
2 cups vegetable stock (p. 22)
1 carrot, sliced
1 celery rib, sliced
1 small zucchini, sliced
½ cup fresh mushrooms, sliced
soy sauce

Combine the barley, stock, carrot, and celery. Bring to a boil, reduce the heat, and simmer for 30 minutes. Add the zucchini and mushrooms and simmer for 15 more minutes. Add the soy sauce to taste.

Variation

Chicken stock (p. 21) or beef stock (p. 20) may be used instead of the vegetable stock. Substitute millet for the barley and cook for the same length of time. Season with ¼ teaspoon crushed rosemary.

Lentil Soup

While many people think that lentils need soaking, the good news is that the brown ones don't. They cook completely in just a half-hour. The recipe here is for lentil soup in its simplest form. Jazz it up with some chopped tomato if you like.

2 tablespoons butter
⅓ onion, chopped
¼ teaspoon curry powder
pinch cayenne
1½ cups water or beef or chicken stock (pp. 20-21)
½ cup lentils, rinsed
pinch salt, optional
3 tablespoons yogurt or sour cream

Melt the butter in the bottom of a saucepan and add the chopped onion, sautéing until the onion is translucent. Add the curry powder and cayenne and stir briefly. Add the liquid and bring to a boil. Add the lentils to this boiling mixture, return it to a boil, and then reduce the heat to a simmer for about 30 minutes. Then taste and add a pinch of salt if desired.

Top with yogurt or sour cream and serve hot.

Cream of Artichoke Soup

Since this is a rich soup, plan on a light salad for accompaniment.

2 teaspoons butter
2 teaspoons unbleached, all-purpose flour
1½ cups milk
1 artichoke bottom, cooked and diced
pinch salt, optional
pinch pepper, optional
1 teaspoon cream sherry, optional
nutmeg, optional

Melt the butter in a skillet. Once the butter has melted, stir in the flour and cook for 1 minute. Add the milk to the flour slowly, stirring constantly with a wire whisk.

Pour about half of the milk mixture into a blender with the artichoke bottom and blend until smooth. Return this mixture to the pan and heat through. Taste; then add salt and pepper if desired. Add the sherry just before serving. For a garnish, you may want just a whisper of nutmeg dusted over this dish.

Borscht

Which is it—cabbage soup or beet soup? It's both. Cook the beets along with the sturdy vegetables, then add the cabbage.

2 tablespoons butter
1 large beet, cubed
1 carrot, sliced
½ onion, diced
2 cups beef stock (p. 20)
1 tablespoon vinegar
½ cup shredded cabbage, red or green
2 tablespoons sour cream

Melt the butter in a soup pot. Sauté all the vegetables (except the cabbage) briefly in the butter. Add the stock and vinegar and bring to a boil, then simmer for about 20 minutes. Check the vegetables for tenderness and cook longer if necessary.

Add the cabbage to the simmering vegetables and cook for about 15 minutes. Serve topped with sour cream.

Pasta e Fagioli

While the name suggests pasta and beans (which translate to "fagioli" in Italian), a strong feature of this soup historically is a hearty ham-bone stock. This offering is surprisingly lusty and flavorful and can be made with or without ham.

Leftover soup can be frozen or stored in the refrigerator for several days.

½ cup diced ham, optional
2 cups cooked red or cranberry beans
3 cups ham stock (p. 19) or water
1 garlic clove
½ onion, chopped
2 carrots, shredded
2 celery ribs, chopped
2 tomatoes, chopped
½ cup small pasta (pastina is preferred)
1 garlic clove, minced
1 tablespoon olive oil
2 tablespoons grated Parmesan or Romano cheese

Simmer everything but the last five ingredients in a soup pot until the vegetables are well cooked and the beans mash easily, about 45 minutes.

Remove the ham bone, then add the tomatoes and pasta. Cook for 20 minutes.

While the soup is cooking, brown the garlic in the olive oil *without* burning it. Pour the hot soup into a soup bowl; float the browned garlic in the center and circle with the grated cheese. Serve immediately.

Paul Escobosa Carrot-Kidney Bean Soup

This subtle soup is a real triumph and an excellent choice for a winter breakfast. This recipe starts from scratch with dried kidney beans. For a shortcut, canned beans will be just as good. Use one 15–16-ounce can of beans with 4 cups of water, instead of the 6 cups indicated when cooking dried beans from scratch.

½ cup dried kidney beans
6 cups water or stock
1 tablespoon butter
1 tablespoon vegetable oil
1 garlic clove, minced
½ onion, chopped
pinch turmeric
pinch cumin
pinch cayenne
1 carrot, grated
1 tomato, diced
2 tablespoons tomato paste
pinch salt
yogurt, optional

In a soup pot bring the beans to a boil in 6 cups of water; then turn off the burner and transfer the beans and their liquid to a large bowl. (You'll need the pot to start the soup.) Let the beans soak for an hour.

In the bottom of the soup pot, melt the butter and add the oil. Brown the garlic slightly, then add the onion and sauté until limp but not brown. Add the spices and stir.

Add the beans and their liquid to the soup pot. Put the grated carrot in the soup pot. Bring to a boil, then reduce the heat to a simmer and cook for 1 hour.

Stir in the tomato and the tomato paste. Cook for an additional 10 minutes. Salt to taste.

Put the soup through a food mill. Be very thorough, and leave as little as possible in the mill. If you don't have a food mill, use a blender or mash the soup with a potato masher. Return the soup to the pot to heat through. Serve hot with a yogurt topping, if desired.

Broccoli Cheese Soup

The vegetarian version of this soup gets its body from the addition of torula yeast to a homemade vegetable stock. The same effect can be achieved by adding a ham bone to the cold water. Reserve any ham to add with the broccoli later on. One half-cup of diced ham is about right.

1 quart water
1 onion, cut in wedges
1 whole clove
1 bay leaf
1 tablespoon minced parsley
¼ teaspoon tarragon
1 carrot, sliced into discs
1 ham bone, optional
1 tablespoon smoked torula yeast (if ham bone is not used)
½ pound fresh broccoli, chopped into small chunks
½ cup diced ham, optional
¼ pound Swiss cheese, grated and dusted with flour

Bring to a boil the water, onion, clove, bay leaf, parsley, tarragon, carrot, and ham bone, if desired. Then simmer for 15 minutes, if no ham bone is added, or for 30 minutes with the ham bone. Strain the soup and return it to the pot.

If you're not using a ham bone, stir the yeast into the broth, add the broccoli and diced ham, if desired, and simmer for 5–6 minutes, until the broccoli is al dente and the ham is heated through.

Gradually add the cheese to the hot soup, stirring constantly. Serve when the cheese has melted.

Succotash Chowder

This recipe is very easy to make from frozen corn and lima beans. Of course, use fresh or canned varieties if they're handier, and try using baby green limas if you can get them.

1 tablespoon butter
½ onion, chopped
1 cup chicken stock (p. 21)
½ cup lima beans, frozen or home-cooked
½ cup corn kernels
1 cup half-and-half
salt and pepper to taste

Melt the butter in a saucepan and sauté the onion until tender. Add the stock, beans, and corn to the sautéed onion. Heat to boiling, then simmer for 10–15 minutes.

Once the vegetables have simmered, add the half-and-half, and heat through. Season to taste, heavy on the pepper!

Pea Soup

Fresh peas are almost impossible to get unless you have a garden, so right off the bat we'll compromise with frozen peas. They, too, are tasty.

1½ cups chicken or vegetable stock (pp. 21-22)
1 small carrot, sliced
1 tablespoon chopped parsley
¾ cup peas
salt and pepper to taste

Bring all the ingredients to a boil, then simmer for about 5 minutes. Place in a blender and whirl until smooth. Season to taste. Serve hot.

Mulligatawney

This terrific East Indian soup uses my favorite spice mixture—garam masala. Lamb is often used in this soup, but here chicken is substituted. The pleasant fragrance of this soup will fill your home and linger there.

Plan ahead by cooking ¼ cup brown rice in ½ cup boiling water. In a heavy saucepan this will take about 40 minutes over low heat.

¼ cup butter
1 small onion, chopped
2 whole cloves
2 bay leaves
1 teaspoon curry powder
½ pound chicken (2–3 chicken breasts)
1 apple, diced into large chunks
4 cups chicken stock (p. 21)
⅓ cup lentils, uncooked
2 tablespoons tomato paste
1 teaspoon garam masala (p. 191)
½ cup cooked brown rice

Melt the butter in the bottom of a large soup pot. Add the chopped onion and sauté until softened. Add the cloves, bay leaves, and curry powder to the onion, stir, smell (enjoy!), then add the chicken.

Sauté the chicken. Add the apple, coat with butter, and allow to sauté briefly. Then add the chicken stock, lentils, and tomato paste. Bring to a boil, then simmer for 30 minutes. Remove the chicken and allow the rest of the ingredients to simmer 40 more minutes.

When the chicken has cooled slightly, bone it and chop it. At the end of the simmering period, remove the bay leaves and cloves and return the chicken to the pot along with the garam masala.

Add the rice to the soup at the last minute, then serve.

Variation

You can make chicken curry by pouring leftover Mulligatawney over a couple of sautéed chicken breasts or thighs. Simmer for about 30 minutes and serve with yogurt and chapattis (p. 50).

Potato Leek Soup

This recipe is a classic because it is both simple and elegant. If you can't get leeks, increase the onion. One leek equals half a medium-sized yellow onion. Have your kettle going—you'll need hot water.

1 leek
¼ cup diced onion
1 tablespoon butter
1 potato, unpeeled, cut in ¼-inch dice
1½ cups hot water
½ teaspoon salt
2 tablespoons butter
1 cup hot milk
½ teaspoon pepper
1 tablespoon fresh parsley, minced

Sauté the leek and the onion in butter in a soup pot until soft. Add the potato, water, and salt and simmer for 25–30 minutes. Check the potato from time to time. It should not cook to the point of deterioration.

Add the butter, hot milk, and pepper and heat through. Garnish with parsley and serve.

➤TO CLEAN A LEEK◄

1. Cut the top off the leek and peel away the outer layers, much as you would a green onion.

2. Cut the leek in half lengthwise. Immerse it in cold water, either in a large bowl or in your sink.

3. Gently fan the leek under water to release any grit caught between the layers.

4. Run it under cold running water until thoroughly rinsed.

5. Slice into ¼-inch lengths for cooking.

Cream of Mushroom Soup

This soup is downright luxurious with its richness of butter and light cream and its generous slices of fresh mushroom.

2 tablespoons minced onion
2 tablespoons butter
1 tablespoon whole wheat flour
2 cups chicken stock (p. 21)
¾–1 cup sliced fresh mushrooms
1 cup half-and-half
pinch salt

In a soup pot, sauté the onion in the melted butter. Add the flour to the onion and allow it to cook for about 30 seconds. Gradually stir the stock into the flour mixture using a wire whisk. Bring the mixture to a boil.

Add the mushrooms to the hot stock and reduce the heat to a simmer. Add half-and-half and let the soup simmer for 15 minutes. Salt to taste and serve.

Cabbage and Caraway Soup

Here's a soup with a surprising kick. The basic liquid is soy milk. When seasoned with soy sauce, it is quite delicious. (You may be pleased to learn that low-salt soy sauce is available.)

⅓ cabbage head, sliced in thin wedges
⅓ cup water
½ cup soy milk
½ teaspoon caraway seed
2 teaspoons soy sauce

Cook the cabbage in the water until it is just beginning to get tender. Add the soy milk and cook to heat through. Finally, add the caraway seed and soy sauce. Stir to mix and serve hot.

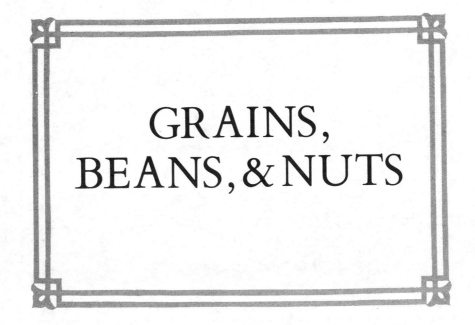

GRAINS, BEANS, & NUTS

These foods, particularly grains and beans, are the staples in the diets of millions of people, many of whom never eat meat at all. This is often out of religious conviction, but often also because of poverty.

We have known for a long time that people can be very healthy living on a grain-and-bean-based vegetarian diet. Now, thanks to a vital interest in vegetarianism here in the United States, nutritionists and lay people have explained in non-technical terms why this is so. Two of the best books on this subject are Lappé's *Diet for a Small Planet* and Robertson, et al.'s *Laurel's Kitchen*.

Always cook grain with a lid. The water-soluble vitamins dissolve in the steam and can escape when the lid is removed. This is particularly true of enriched rice, since the vitamins and minerals are added as a coating to the rice and are easily rinsed away. Cook rice in just the amount of liquid to be absorbed, so no liquid is lost, taking vitamins with it. Use long-grain brown rice when possible.

Rice Pilaf

1–2 PORTIONS

A pilaf is a grain dish (usually rice or barley) cooked according to a special technique that produces an excellent texture. To add interest to the dish, various foods such as raisins, nuts, or sliced mushrooms can be combined with the cooked grain.

1 teaspoon vegetable oil
½ cup brown rice
1 cup broth (chicken or beef)

Heat the oil in a heavy saucepan and add the rice to it. Stir until the rice is toasted light brown. Then, without stirring, add the broth, reduce the heat to very low, and cover. Cook for 40 minutes. All the broth should be absorbed, and the rice should be plump, each grain separate.

⇒SINGLE SERVINGS OF GRAIN⇐

Grain Type	Yield and Time
Barley, hulled—not pearled. (Pearled barley is not a whole grain. Some of the outer coating has been removed, along with some nutrients.)	⅓ cup cooked in 1 cup liquid yields 1 cup in 1 hour.
Brown rice (not enriched or converted)	½ cup cooked in 1 cup liquid yields 1½–1¾ cups in 40 minutes.
Buckwheat groats (kasha)	½ cup cooked in 1 cup liquid yields 1⅓ cups in 12-15 minutes.
Millet	⅓ cup cooked in 1 cup liquid yields 1 cup in 40 minutes.
Cornmeal, polenta-grade desirable	⅓ cup cooked in 1 cup liquid yields 1 cup in 20 minutes.
Bulghur wheat	½ cup cooked in 1 cup liquid yields 1¼ cups in 15 minutes.

Soubise

1 PORTION

This is a rice-and-onion casserole you won't forget. The onion is sautéed, but not completely tamed. Use a good Swiss cheese if you can. If not, the garden variety will do.

Use leftover cooked rice or simmer ¼ cup long-grain brown rice in ½ cup broth for 40 minutes.

1 yellow onion, sliced thin
2 tablespoons butter
½ cup cooked rice
pinch salt
pinch pepper
2 tablespoons grated Swiss cheese

Preheat the oven to 325° F.
Sauté the onion in 1½ tablespoons of the melted butter until it is limp. Stir in the rice. Salt and pepper to taste. Cover and bake for 45 minutes. Stir in the cheese and the remaining ½ tablespoon butter. Serve.

Risotto alla Milanese

Risotto is a familiar Italian side dish. It requires some attention, but you can take a shortcut and cook the rice all at once, if you wish. The remaining ingredients can be tossed in later.

1 tablespoon minced onion
1 tablespoon butter
½ cup long-grain brown rice
1 cup chicken stock (p. 21)
pinch saffron
1½ tablespoons grated Parmesan cheese

Sauté the onion in butter in a saucepan. Add the rice. Cover with ¼ cup of the stock. Simmer until the rice absorbs the liquid, stirring constantly. Add another ¼ cup stock, and stir again until the liquid is absorbed. Repeat until the final ¼ cup is added. Continue to stir until the rice is tender.

Add the saffron, stir in the Parmesan cheese, and serve.

Quick Risotto

Add the liquid to the onion all at once and bring to a boil. Add the rice, cover, and cook over very low heat for 40 minutes. Stir in the saffron and Parmesan. Serve.

Variations

- Sautéed mushrooms may be added during the final stirring stage (this is called Risotto al Funghi).
- Finely chopped cooked chicken liver or gizzard may be added if available.

Ginger Rice Casserole

I'm always looking for an excuse to mince fresh ginger. This is a great one. You'll need some leftover beef or chicken to round out this dish.

1 garlic clove, minced
½ teaspoon minced ginger
2 tablespoons vegetable oil
2 tablespoons finely chopped green pepper
1 teaspoon soy sauce
1½ cups chicken stock (p. 21)
¾ cup long-grain brown rice
½ cup chopped cooked beef or chicken
1 green onion, chopped

Sauté the garlic and ginger in the hot oil for 15 seconds or so. Add the green pepper and sauté until soft.

Add the soy sauce and chicken stock and bring to a boil. Reduce the heat. Add the rice, and cook with the lid on for 25 minutes. Add the chopped meat, stir once, and continue cooking with the lid on for another 20 minutes. Toss with the green onion and serve.

Barley Pilaf

I love the chewiness of barley. It is both mellow and robust, and it marries beautifully with sautéed mushrooms and sage. Try your own variations in addition to the ones listed.

Select a pan with a lid that can go into the oven, or have a greased, 2-cup individual casserole dish ready and cover it with foil for baking.

1 tablespoon vegetable oil
½ onion, cut in large dice
8–10 medium-sized mushrooms, sliced
1 cup chicken or beef stock (p. 20–21)
⅓ cup whole barley, hulled
2 tablespoons wheat germ or chopped walnuts
2 teaspoons sage

Preheat the oven to 350° F.

Heat the oil over medium heat. Add the diced onion. Sauté until tender. Add the sliced mushrooms and continue to sauté until the mushrooms are tender.

Pour the stock into the pan and bring to a boil. Reduce the heat. Add the barley, wheat germ, and sage. Cover (or transfer to a casserole dish and cover). Bake for 1 hour. Uncover for the final 10 minutes of baking. Serve.

Variations

- Rice or millet can be added instead of barley. Bake for 45 minutes.
- ¼ cup grated carrot is good in addition to the mushrooms.
- ¾ cup broccoli florets can be added at the baking step.
- ⅓ cup grated cheese can be folded into the finished casserole.
- Omit the mushrooms and sage. Add ½ teaspoon curry powder, ¼ cup raisins, and ¼ cup walnuts. (Chopped apple may be substituted for raisins.)

➔FACELESS LEFTOVER GRAIN CASSEROLE◄

Combine cooked grain with grated raw vegetables or chopped cooked vegetables. Add enhancers such as wheat germ, soy grits, chopped nuts, or breadcrumbs. Bind the mixture with a beaten egg and some milk. Flavor with celery salt, sage, soy sauce, or curry powder, for just a few examples.

Fold in some grated cheese, such as cheddar, Swiss, or Parmesan. Top with breadcrumbs or grated Parmesan cheese and bake at 350° F. for 1 hour.

Top with Cashew Sauce (p. 181), Basic Cheese Sauce (p. 177), or a tomato sauce.

Tabouleh

This warm grain salad is made with bulghur wheat and is a tasty companion to lentil soup or a lamb chop. It is good warm or cold and improves with time.

Tabouleh will keep for up to two weeks in the refrigerator. The tomato will tell you when its time is up!

1 cup water
½ cup bulghur wheat
⅛ teaspoon salt
1 small tomato, chopped
2 teaspoons olive oil
1 green onion, chopped, or 1 tablespoon chopped chives
2 tablespoons chopped parsley
juice of ½ lemon
⅛ teaspoon dried mint

Bring the water to a boil. Add the bulghur and salt, reduce the heat, and simmer over very low heat for 15 minutes.

Once the liquid is absorbed by the bulghur, add the remaining ingredients. Toss and serve.

Polenta

Polenta is as prominent on some Northern Italian tables as potatoes are on American tables. It is a cornmeal mush made with a coarsely ground, undegermed cornmeal and is ideally suited to meaty winter meals. A stewed joint, a braised shank, broiled fish, and sausage all complement polenta well.

A good polenta is a creamy, glistening, and thick yellow mush that sets when cold. The key problem in making polenta is that it can lump. The only precautions have to do with how to avoid this.

½ teaspoon salt
1 cup water or broth
⅓ cup cornmeal
2 tablespoons pan drippings or gravy, optional

Add the salt to the water in a heavy saucepan. Then *very slowly* pour the cornmeal into the salted liquid. You will need to stir *constantly* throughout this preparation. Turn on the burner and heat the mixture. Do not bring to a boil. Stir constantly. Simmer until the polenta leaves the sides of the pan. This will take about 20 minutes. Stir in the pan drippings or gravy. Serve immediately.

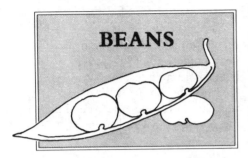

BEANS

Think of protein when you think of beans! The texture and substance make them a good main dish. They accept seasoning marvelously, and by adding a little cheese, meat, or rice, you'll have a tasty meal that contains the complete protein you need.

Black beans, black-eyed peas, garbanzo beans, great northerns, kidney beans, lima beans, baby lima beans, navy beans, pinto beans, red beans, and small white beans can be dried. They will keep for over a year if stored in jars in a cool place.

Dried beans must be soaked before they are cooked. Once soaked, plan on an hour or more of cooking. One-half cup of dried beans will yield 1½-2½ cups of cooked beans.

Thanks go to the California Bean Advisory Board for these soaking methods.

One-hour hot soak. In a saucepan, cover ½ cup dried beans with 4 cups hot water. Bring to a boil. Boil for 2 minutes, then turn off the heat and let sit for 1 hour. The beans will then be ready to cook.

Overnight salt soak. The salt in this method permits more even absorption of water. In a saucepan, cover ½ cup dried beans with 4 cups hot water. Add ½ teaspoon salt, and stir. Let stand overnight. If you are a working person, you can soak the beans overnight and cook them in the morning while you're getting ready for work. If you don't want to add the salt, you don't have to.

Soybeans are the only legumes that contain a complete protein. Unlike other beans, though, soybeans require prolonged cooking after soaking. In a heavy saucepan, place soybeans and water in a ratio of 1 part soybeans to 3 parts cold water. Bring the mixture to a boil, reduce the heat to a gentle simmer, cover loosely, and simmer for 3½ hours. During the last hour of cooking you may need to add more water. Adjust the taste with about 1 teaspoon soy sauce or ¼ teaspoon salt per cup of soybeans.

Basic Beans

During cooking the bean pot can be loaded with flavorful morsels that create different savory results. This recipe represents one idea.

2 cups soaked beans in their liquid
1 cup broth or water
1 whole onion
3 whole cloves
6–8 peppercorns
½ teaspoon dry mustard
1 bay leaf
1 tablespoon vegetable oil
2–3 whole garlic cloves
¼ teaspoon salt

Leave the beans in their soaking liquid and supplement that liquid with the broth. Pierce the onion with the whole cloves and add to the beans. Add the remaining ingredients and cook for 1½ hours, until the beans are tender but not mushy. Discard the onion, cloves, peppercorns, garlic, and bay leaf, and serve.

Refried Beans Picante

"Picante" is Spanish for hot. This recipe could also be called "Spicy Refried Beans." Mexican salsa is a hot sauce that you can buy in the Mexican-food section of most supermarkets.

1 tablespoon chopped onion
2 teaspoons butter, melted
⅛ teaspoon cumin
½ 16-ounce can refried beans
1 tablespoon grated cheese (Jack or cheddar)
1–2 teaspoons Mexican salsa

Sauté the chopped onion in a small frying pan with the melted butter. Add the cumin. Stir briefly, then add the half-can of refried beans. Stir to heat through, then add the grated cheese and salsa. Stir again until the cheese is melted.

Quick Chili con Carne

You can make this mild dish really hot by adding Mexican salsa picante or some cayenne, but remember—there's no turning back!

¼ pound ground chuck
¼ onion, diced
1 garlic clove, minced
2 teaspoons mild chili powder
⅛ teaspoon cumin
2 tablespoons diced green pepper, optional
1 tomato, diced
1 8½-ounce can kidney beans, drained
grated sharp cheddar cheese, optional

Brown the ground chuck in a skillet. Move to one side. Sauté the onion and garlic in the fat of the hamburger. Add the chili powder, cumin, and green pepper and stir for 30 seconds.

Add the diced tomato. Cook for 2 minutes. Then pour in the kidney beans. Heat through, about 15 minutes.

Top with grated sharp cheddar cheese, if desired, and serve.

Limas con Chiles y Queso

This recipe is modified from one provided by the California Bean Advisory Board. It makes good use of the naturally buttery quality of limas, while the chilies and cheddar give the dish a zippy Mexican flavor. Choose a 4-ounce can of mild chilies and use the leftover chilies in frittatas or casseroles over the next couple of weeks. Keep the peppers in the refrigerator once the can has been opened. Select an individual casserole dish to hold 1½ cups.

1¼ cups cooked lima beans
2 tablespoons chopped mild chilies
½ cup grated cheddar cheese
3 tablespoons liquid from lima beans
2 tablespoons sour cream

Preheat the oven to 350° F.

Divide the beans, cheese, and chilies in half and layer in the casserole dish: beans, chilies, cheddar. The second layer should be topped with cheddar. Combine the bean liquid and the sour cream, and pour the mixture over the casserole. Bake uncovered for 30 minutes. Serve hot.

Lima Beans Neufchâtel

This French bean dish is very delicate, with a tender milk and egg sauce reminiscent of mild Neufchâtel cheese.

This method of preparing lima beans makes a great hot lunch or dinner with a piece of fruit and a glass of juice.

½ cup milk
2 egg yolks, slightly beaten
1 tablespoon butter, melted and cooled
1 cup cooked lima beans
⅛ teaspoon salt

Preheat the oven to 350° F.

Make a mixture of the milk, egg yolk, and melted butter. Put the lima beans into an individual casserole dish, add the salt and the egg mixture. Place in the preheated oven and bake for 30 minutes, stirring occasionally as it bakes. Remove from the oven and serve hot.

Curried Pease Pudding

This is a lovely way to present any bean dish. The curry powder makes yellow split peas even more vivid. The mixture is steamed in a pudding mold and is served unmolded in a generous bed of sour cream.

The first step of this two-phase project is to make a plain split pea mush, which is the "pease porridge hot" of the children's nursery rhyme. It is rather dull, which is why we take the next step: adding curry powder.

½ cup dried yellow split peas, rinsed and picked clean
¼ teaspoon salt
2 cups water
1 tablespoon butter
pinch pepper
1 egg, slightly beaten
2 teaspoons curry powder
⅓ cup sour cream

Cover the dried split peas with salted water and bring to a boil. Reduce the heat and simmer for 40 minutes. The peas should be tender. Stir in the butter and pepper. Allow the mixture to cool slightly, then stir in the beaten egg and the curry powder.

Turn into an oiled pudding mold of 2-cup capacity. The pudding will swell during cooking so leave about 2 inches of space at the top. Cover the pudding mold and place it inside a cooking pot filled with water about halfway up the side of the pudding mold. Steam with both the pudding mold and the steaming pot covered, on top of the stove, for 45 minutes. Invert the pudding onto a serving plate and serve with sour cream.

Marinated Garbanzo Bean Salad

This salad gets better with age, and it's delicious to begin with! I like to make it from scratch, but certain brands of canned beans are perfectly fine to use. (Check the ingredient listing on the can to determine whether additives or excess salt are present.) Because of the marinade, the salad will keep nicely for two weeks in a covered container in the refrigerator. The size of the salad can vary greatly, so note the proportions I use and adapt them accordingly.

½ cup dried garbanzo beans
4 cups water
⅓ cup olive oil
¼ teaspoon thyme
¼ teaspoon basil
1 small garlic clove, minced
1 tablespoon finely chopped onion
2 tablespoons vinegar
1 tablespoon lemon juice
10–12 torn cilantro leaves
2 tablespoons chopped fresh parsley
1 tomato, cut into small dice
6–8 small mushroom caps

Cook the beans according to the "one-hour hot soak" method outlined at the beginning of this chapter (p. 38).

Bathe the cooked beans in the olive oil. Then add the herbs, garlic, and onion. Toss to distribute, then add the remaining ingredients and toss again. Marinate overnight and then serve.

❧ BEAN SANDWICH SPREADS ❧

Here are a few ways you can make good use of leftover cooked beans. Bean sprouts and tomato or cucumber slices will add moisture and textural interest and will add up to a very nutritious and tasty meal. Pita bread is good for this type of sandwich since you can include more vegetables.

- Refried beans mixed with Mexican salsa and minced onion.
- Mashed lima beans mixed with mayonnaise and mustard.
- Kidney beans mashed with Mexican salsa and grated cheddar cheese.
- Mashed beans served with sliced red onion and lettuce.

NUTS

Nuts and seeds offer a rich supply of plant protein, B vitamins, and unsaturated fats. However, bringing a good balance of quality nuts and seeds into the diet takes some extra effort. Stock your kitchen with ¼ pound each of almonds, walnuts, cashews, and raw peanuts, and make a habit of including chopped nuts in your casseroles and salads. For example, try a watercress-endive salad with walnuts and chopped apples, topped with a piece of chèvre and a vinaigrette dressing. Garnish your desserts with whole almonds. Snack on cashews and try putting peanuts in your rice.

Seeds are as easy to keep as nuts. Sesame seeds and sunflower seeds, for example, can be treated like wheat germ, kept in a sealed jar in the refrigerator and used as a booster in cereals, salads, and grain casseroles.

Nut-Mushroom Burritos

1–2 BURRITOS

While you're making the filling, the tortillas can be warming in foil in a low oven. To make the burrito even richer, add some sliced avocado.

6–10 small-to-medium mushrooms, sliced
1 tablespoon butter
2 tablespoons chopped walnuts
2 tablespoons grated Swiss cheese
2 tablespoons sour cream
2 warm flour tortillas

Preheat the oven to 250° F.

Sauté the mushrooms in the butter. Add the walnuts and allow them to heat through. Then add the cheese and stir. Turn off the burner.

Spread the sour cream in the center of the warm tortillas (1 tablespoon for each tortilla). Add the nut-mushroom mixture to the center of each tortilla, fold, and serve.

BREADSTUFFS

People make their own bread because it is satisfying to body and soul, and because it is economical. This chapter covers a broad selection of breads—unleavened (made without yeast) and leavened.

Unleavened breads must have been developed by people in a hurry, and they have remained popular because people are still in a hurry. These breads are essentially flour and water with minor variations, and they are easily adapted to small serving sizes. Most recipes are made on top of the stove.

When you are baking with yeast, on the other hand, you are working with a living thing—coaxing it, conquering it, unleashing its power. Yeast breads take much longer, mainly because of the time you must allow for rising, but the result is *always* worth the time and effort.

CRÊPES

Crêpes are known by various names depending on the country where they're made. I was raised to think of crêpes as *egguponak-aka* since that's what my Norwegian grandmother always made. My Hungarian friend calls his crêpes *palacsinta*. Each recipe is just a little different, yielding a thinner, sturdier, or smoother result. I have synthesized my recipe, using what I consider to be the better qualities of each. The result is a thin yet strong crêpe that is easy to make and delicate when eaten.

If possible, plan ahead and refrigerate the batter for a couple of hours. This is not essential, but butter is more evenly suspended in chilled batter, and you will notice a greater ease of handling.

Next, if you give care to the pan before you start, you'll save yourself much grief. Your choice should be a seasoned cast-iron frying pan or crêpe pan. Some of the new treated aluminum cookware also works well if properly seasoned. (To season a pan, oil it generously, heat it for about 4 minutes, allow it to cool for 5–10 minutes, wipe away the excess oil, and proceed. You will still need to butter the pan before you begin.)

Basic Crêpes

Five or six crêpes are a good amount for breakfast if they are buttered and lightly coated with jelly. At dinner, the amount one can eat depends on the amount of filling used. If filled with one asparagus spear, six crêpes can be consumed with ease. If there is leftover crêpe batter, it may be refrigerated for up to three days.

Also, crêpes may be frozen. I often make all the crêpes at once and freeze those I won't fill right away. Separate the crêpes with plastic wrap to prevent them from sticking. Finally, filled crêpes can be either refrigerated for up to three days, or frozen if the filling will hold up.

This recipe can be doubled or tripled using a ratio of 1 egg to 1 cup of milk (which will produce a lighter crêpe than the single recipe). Don't double the salt though—⅛ teaspoon is the most you should add.

2 tablespoons unbleached, all-purpose flour
⅛ teaspoon salt
1 egg, slightly beaten
½ cup milk
1 tablespoon butter, melted and cooled

Add the flour and salt to the egg. Gradually stir in the milk with a wire whisk. Lastly, add the cooled, melted butter. Chill the batter if convenient.

Heat the seasoned pan over a medium flame, butter it lightly, and then reduce the heat to medium-low.

Pour about 2 tablespoons of batter into the heated pan. Grasp the handle of the pan (with a hotpad if need be!) and tilt the pan surface so that the batter flows into a pancake shape. As you do this, the batter should begin to set. Once the pan is back on the burner and the batter is no longer runny, the crêpe can be turned. You can use a spatula to loosen the rim of the crêpe from the pan before turning it. If the crêpe bunches a little, simply flatten it.

The crêpe is ready when the second side is lightly browned. This should take 20–30 seconds. Turn the crêpe onto a warm plate—crêpes can be stacked on top of one another without sticking. If you're worried about this, layer plastic wrap in between the crêpes, but don't put them into the oven this way.

Before starting the second crêpe, swirl the batter to reintegrate the butter.

⇒CRÊPE FILLING IDEAS⇐

Once you have made the crêpes, there is an unlimited number of fillings and toppings you can use to round out the dish. What's listed here is a cross-section of these choices so your imagination will be sparked to use whatever you have on hand. Leftovers are a prime candidate for crêpe filling. All you need to do is make a sauce to dress them up.

Dessert Crêpes

- Sauté an apple in butter, then sweeten it in the pan with some honey. (Less than a tablespoon of honey is needed for 1 apple.) Spice this mixture with some cinnamon and cook until soft. Use this as a crêpe filling, then top with whipping cream or Crème Fraîche (p. 177). Serve hot.
- Soak fresh berries in a liqueur, fold into sour cream, and stuff in a crêpe!

Breakfast Crêpes

- Serve the crêpe plain and hot topped with butter and your favorite syrup or jam.
- Wrap a crêpe around some eggs and top with Mexican salsa.

Main-Dish Crêpes

- Fill with ratatouille and top with a tomato sauce.
- Wrap asparagus in a crêpe and top with a creamy cheese sauce.
- Fill the crêpe with your favorite steamed vegetable, then top with a cream sauce of shrimp or crab and some white wine. Bake for about 10 minutes at 325° F.
- Fill with Chinese vegetables (featuring water chestnuts) topped with a light, soy-flavored vegetable sauce.
- Mix some ricotta cheese, an egg, and some fresh (or frozen and drained) spinach with a touch of nutmeg and grated Parmesan cheese. Stuff each crêpe with 2 tablespoons of this, then top with a rich tomato sauce and bake for half an hour at 325° F.

I think this is the easiest flat bread to make. It is traditionally eaten in India, often taking the place of silverware as a means of scooping up various foods. And it's a staple in the diet of the Hunzakut—a people living in the Himalayas whose eating habits we would do well to emulate! Make these chapatti at the last minute and serve hot. Three chapatti are roughly equivalent to two pieces of bread.

½ cup whole wheat flour
pinch salt
2 teaspoons vegetable oil
2 tablespoons water

Combine all the ingredients and work the dough with your hands until it holds together. Add a few more drops of water if necessary. When the dough is firm, knead it on a board for about 4 minutes.

Divide the dough into thirds, and roll each third into a 5–7-inch circle. Have a 7-inch cast-iron skillet medium hot. Don't butter the pan—this bread is cooked dry. Put the first chapattis in the pan and cook it for about 30 seconds. Then turn, and allow the second side to cook for 15–20 more seconds.

In cooking, air pockets will form, causing the chapattis to balloon. Don't pop the bubble, as the bread will dehydrate. Remove the cooked chapattis to a serving plate and butter immediately. Keep warm until all three chapatti are done; then serve.

TORTILLAS

The tortilla is a Mexican bread which combines the familiar ingredients of flour, fat, and water to produce a variation on flat breads found all over the world. The recipes provided in this section assume the tortilla will be fresh or thawed from frozen.

The drawback to cooking tortillas for one person is that they are usually sold in packages of a dozen or more. To make the best use of that quantity, separate the tortillas into groups of two or three and freeze them. If they were frozen when you bought them, try to pry loose only those which you intend to use, so the entire package doesn't have to be thawed and used in a short time.

Flour Tortillas

Flour tortillas are very good plain or lightly buttered. They can be heated either by steaming them, or by warming them in the oven in a closed container. Eat them as you would bread, with any meal. The flour tortilla is the more refined and pliable of the two types.

Because it handles so easily and because of its width (about 10 inches), the flour tortilla is ideal for wrapping beans, cheeses, meats, rice, and vegetables into many variations of the burrito. Burritos freeze beautifully, so you can make up a batch and have several future meals on hand to reheat.

Corn Tortillas

The corn tortilla is smaller and more substantial than the flour tortilla. It behaves in different ways, depending on how it is cooked. When fried in hot oil, it becomes crisp and can be folded or kept flat to support a range of ingredients used in tostadas or tacos. If the tortilla is baked without having been fried, it will become crispy but will be more dry. Also, the tortilla can be torn into small pieces and added to a casserole. Finally, enchiladas are an excellent freeze-ahead meal which will use up a whole package of corn tortillas in one batch.

To fry corn tortillas. Put about ⅛ inch vegetable oil in a frying pan and heat over a medium-high flame. The oil must be fresh and hot to minimize the absorption of fats while the tortilla is frying and to avoid the development of off flavors.

For tostadas, tacos, or tortilla chips, place the tortilla or tortilla pieces in the hot oil for just a few seconds—10 to 15 seconds at the most. Then, turn with tongs and, if you are making folded taco shells, fold the tortilla in half while it is still in the pan.

Cook the tortilla on the second side for 10 to 15 seconds. Remove to paper towels to drain.

To bake corn tortillas. Preheat your oven to 350° F. Tortillas can be baked instead of fried when you are making tostadas or tortilla chips. For tostadas, spread the tortilla with refried beans and grated cheese and place it on a cookie sheet. Bake for 5 minutes; then remove and add topping ingredients (see One-Step Tostada, p. 53). To make tortilla chips, cut the tortillas into wedge-shaped pieces, place them on a cookie sheet, and bake until the tortilla chips have reached the desired crispness—about 10 minutes.

To make nachos. When corn tortillas have begun to get a little old and dry, it is an excellent time to make up a batch of nachos. First, make up some tortilla chips, either by frying them until golden or baking them until they have the desired crispness. Preheat your oven to 350° F. Place the chips on a cookie sheet and grate Jack or cheddar cheese over them. Bake for 5 to 6 minutes. Eat with any dip, particularly with a hot peppery tomato dip or Guacamole (p. 79).

One-Step Tostada

Whether two tostadas make one or two portions depends on how hungry you are. If you want to save a tostada for reheating, it may be refrigerated for a couple of days. Freezing is successful if only the tortilla, beans, cheese, and rice are frozen. Add the vegetables when fresh and ready to be eaten, since they deteriorate when frozen.

4 tablespoons cooked rice, optional
5 tablespoons Refried Beans Picante (p. 39) or plain refried beans
2 corn tortillas
2 tablespoons grated cheese (Jack or cheddar)
1 tablespoon finely chopped green onion
½ tomato, chopped
⅓ cup shredded lettuce
2 tablespoons sour cream
Mexican salsa

Combine the rice with the refried beans, divide in half, and spread on the corn tortillas. Sprinkle the cheese over the bean mixture. Place in the oven on a cookie sheet, turn the oven to 350° F., and heat until the cheese has melted—about 5 minutes. Remove the tortillas to a plate and top with the chopped vegetables, sour cream, and salsa. Eat the tostada with your hands!

Scrambled Egg Tostada

While you're scrambling the eggs, let the tortilla and cheese heat through in the oven.

2 tablespoons grated cheese (Jack or cheddar)
1 corn tortilla
2 eggs
2 tablespoons milk or cream
1 teaspoon butter
2 teaspoons chopped jalapeño peppers
1 tablespoon sour cream
pinch salt
pinch pepper
avocado slices, optional

Place the cheese on the tortilla and place it in the oven. Turn the oven to 350° F.; there is no need to preheat it. Beat the eggs with a wire whisk and add the milk, beating until well incorporated. Melt the butter in a frying pan. Turn the eggs into the frying pan and stir gently from the bottom of the pan until the eggs are set.

Remove the heated tortilla from the oven, and spoon the scrambled egg over the melted cheese on the tortilla. Top with jalapeño peppers, sour cream, salt, and pepper.

Leftover Cereal Bread

This recipe and the one that follows are adapted from recipes that appear in The Tassajara Bread Book.

These are heavy, earthy, and nourishing loaves made without leavening. Make this dough using your leftover cooked cereal, then let it sit overnight. Bake the bread in the morning—it's a perfect breakfast bread, especially in the wintertime.

1 tablespoon vegetable oil, optional
¼ teaspoon salt
½ cup leftover cooked cereal
1½ cups whole wheat flour
¼ cup chopped nuts, dates, or raisins, optional

Combine the oil and salt with the cooked cereal. Add the flour gradually up to 1 cup. The dough should be slightly moist. With the remaining ½ cup flour, dust your kneading board. Knead the dough 300 times, gradually working in the flour. Once well mixed, add the nuts, dates, or raisins, if desired, and continue to knead for the remainder of the 300 strokes. The dough should become increasingly smooth and be firm, yet pliable.

Shape the kneaded dough into a loaf and place it in an oiled and floured mini-loaf pan (6"x3¼"x2") or a straight-sided baking dish with a 1½-cup capacity. Cut a ½-inch slit down the length of the loaf top, brush with water, and cover with a moist towel. Let the dough sit in a warm place overnight.

Bake at 350° F. for 65-75 minutes. Remove baked bread from the pan and cool. To soften crust, butter it and/or cover it with a clean dishtowel while it cools.

❧TASSAJARA❧

Tassajara is a valley in Monterrey County where the San Francisco Zen Center owns a Buddhist monastery which serves as a retreat. Edward Espe Brown, who was a cook at the monastery, wrote *The Tassajara Bread Book,* which became a best seller, along with his *Tassajara Cooking.* Here in San Francisco there is a Tassajara Bakery where one can buy truly outstanding healthful and tasty baked goods. I have Edward Brown's kind permission to use these recipes and they are very dear to my heart.

Gruel Bread

The Gruel Bread recipe does seem a little fantastic, yet it appeals to me enormously as a means of using every scrap of leftovers possible, and making crackers, to boot. Use any leftover grain or vegetable combination, and you will have the basis for this bread, another offering of The Tassajara Bread Book. *A few remaining bites of rice, a day-old salad, or half a stuffed zucchini will all neatly fit the requirements of Gruel Bread. The lesson here is that flour and water (moisture) plus time (the dough sits overnight) will create something tasty from almost any combination of foods. These recipes taught me a lot about bread making. My most recent Gruel Bread featured leftover refried beans mixed with some cooked carrots.*

1 tablespoon vegetable oil, optional
¼ teaspoon salt or soy sauce
⅔ cup gruel
1 cup whole wheat flour

Combine the oil (if desired) and salt with the gruel. Add the flour gradually up to ⅔ cup. The dough should be slightly moist. With the remaining ⅓ cup flour, dust your kneading board. Knead the dough 300 times, gradually working in the flour. The dough should become increasingly smooth and be firm, yet pliable.

Shape the kneaded dough into a loaf and place it in an oiled and floured mini-loaf pan (6"x3¼"x2") or a straight-sided baking dish with a 1½-cup capacity. Cut a ½-inch slit down the length of the loaf top, brush it with water, and cover with a moist towel. Let the dough sit in a warm place overnight.

Bake at 350° F. for 65–75 minutes. Remove baked bread from the pan and cool. To soften crust, butter it and/or cover it with a clean dish-towel while it cools.

Variation

To make crackers, bake thin slices of the *baked* bread on a cookie sheet in a 350° F. oven for 10 minutes. Turn them after about 5 minutes. When the crackers are done, cool them on a rack, and they will become crisp.

Basic Whole Wheat Pancakes

This is a mainstay pancake recipe. It can be varied by partially substituting different flours, changing the dairy products, adding fruits or nuts, and varying the toppings.

If you can't use all the batter now, make the pancakes, and freeze them. You can also store leftover batter in the refrigerator for a couple of days. You'll see some discoloration on the surface of the batter. Just stir it in—it doesn't affect the quality of the batter. ❧

¾ **cup whole wheat flour**
⅛ **teaspoon salt**
1 **egg, slightly beaten**
¾ **cup milk**
1 **teaspoon vegetable oil**
1 **teaspoon baking soda**
1 **tablespoon brown sugar, optional**

Put the flour and salt in a small mixing bowl and add the egg and about half the milk to it. Mix thoroughly, then add the remaining ingredients and stir until mixed.

Heat a skillet and add just enough oil to coat the pan. Spoon the batter onto the hot skillet and cook on the first side until the bubbles that form begin to burst—about 1 minute.

Turn the pancake and cook for about 1½ minutes. Serve.

Oatmeal Pancakes

You can split an egg in half and follow the recipe provided, which will yield six pancakes, or double it for twelve. (Don't double the baking soda though—just use 1½ teaspoons.)

An egg is about 2 tablespoons in volume. To split it, just beat the egg in a small bowl with a fork, then measure 1 tablespoon into the pancake mixture. Add the extra egg to another egg, add some milk, and have scrambled eggs with your pancakes.

Once the oatmeal is added to the batter, it improves with waiting, since the oatmeal then softens somewhat and makes a cakier pancake. ❧

⅓ **cup whole wheat flour**
3 **tablespoons rolled oats**
1 **teaspoon baking soda**
pinch salt
½ **egg**
¾ **cup buttermilk**
1 **tablespoon vegetable oil**

Combine the dry ingredients, then add the liquid ingredients to them. Add the oil last.

Ladle or pour the pancakes onto a hot griddle. Turn when the tiny bubbles forming on the pancakes begin to burst—about 1 minute. Cook for about 1½ minutes on the second side. Serve hot.

MUFFINS

Muffins are as easy to make as pancakes—easier when you consider that you don't have to stand over them with a spatula in hand. All these muffins are a little on the heavy side, but they are intended to be more nutritious than the quickbreads which follow. If you want a lighter muffin, substitute unbleached, all-purpose flour for the whole wheat flour I have listed.

The recipes provided are for six muffins if muffin tins are used, or for four if individual custard cups are used.

Don't overbeat muffin batter because that will produce a heavy, tough result. To assure that this won't happen, always assemble the liquid ingredients and add them to the dry ingredients which have been mixed in a separate bowl.

There is really no need to use paper liners. Oil the tin or custard cup, and the muffin will twist out once it has cooled slightly.

If you are baking only a few muffins in your muffin tins, put water in the vacant spaces to prevent scorching.

Granola Muffins

4–6 MUFFINS

For best results, the batter for these muffins should be made the night before. The texture improves once the granola has absorbed the moisture. Batter can be stored in the refrigerator for up to one week. When ready to bake, oil and flour as many containers as you will need.

½ cup granola
½ cup whole wheat flour
1½ teaspoons baking powder
pinch salt, optional
½ cup fruit juice
2 tablespoons honey
1 egg, slightly beaten
1 tablespoon vegetable oil

Combine the dry ingredients in a mixing bowl. Mix the liquid ingredients in a separate bowl, then add them to the dry. Stir briefly to mix, then refrigerate overnight.

Preheat the oven to 400° F.

Fill the muffin tins ¾ full and place in the preheated oven. Bake for 20–25 minutes. The muffins are done when a toothpick inserted into the center comes out clean.

Apple Raisin Muffins

This favorite recipe is as special as a Christmas cake, but much easier to make. The muffins are very moist, with an excellent texture. The batter can be stored in the refrigerator for up to 48 hours. Oil and flour as many containers as you intend to use.

¾ cup whole wheat flour
½ teaspoon baking soda
1 tablespoon wheat germ
⅛ teaspoon salt
¼ teaspoon nutmeg
½ apple, chopped fine
¼ cup raisins
1 egg, slightly beaten
1½ tablespoons honey
⅓ cup milk
2 teaspoons vegetable oil

Preheat the oven to 400° F.

Combine the dry ingredients in a mixing bowl. Add the apple and raisins to the flour mixture. Combine the liquid ingredients in a separate bowl, then add them to the dry, stirring briefly to avoid overbeating.

Fill each muffin container ¾ full and place in the preheated oven. Bake for 25 minutes. The muffins are done when a toothpick inserted into the center comes out clean.

Variations

Try cardamom or allspice instead of nutmeg.

You may use 2 tablespoons brown sugar instead of the honey, but add it to the dry ingredients.

Peanut Butter Muffins

The peanut butter in these muffins contributes a distinct but subtle flavor. I enjoy them without jam, but of course jam does come to mind....

The batter can be stored in the refrigerator for up to 48 hours. Oil and flour as many containers as you intend to use.

¾ cup whole wheat flour
1½ teaspoons baking powder
1 tablespoon wheat germ
1 tablespoon honey
2 tablespoons peanut butter
1 egg, slightly beaten
¼ cup milk
1 tablespoon vegetable oil

Preheat the oven to 400° F.

Combine the dry ingredients in a mixing bowl. Mix the liquid ingredients in a separate bowl, then add them to the dry, stirring briefly to avoid overbeating.

Fill each muffin cup ¾ full and place in the preheated oven. Bake for 25 minutes. The muffins are done when a toothpick inserted into the center comes out clean.

Oat and Yogurt Muffins

In this recipe you make your own oat flour. Just put the dry oatmeal in a blender and whirl! Oil and flour as many containers as you plan to use.

½ cup whole wheat flour
¼ cup oat flour
½ teaspoon baking soda
⅛ teaspoon salt
2 tablespoons brown sugar
1 egg, slightly beaten
1 tablespoon vegetable oil
½ cup yogurt

Preheat the oven to 400° F.

Combine the dry ingredients in a mixing bowl. Mix the liquid ingredients and add them to the dry, stirring briefly to avoid overbeating.

Fill each muffin container ¾ full and place in the preheated oven. Bake for 25 minutes. The muffins are done when a toothpick inserted into the center comes out clean.

Variations

Try substituting cornmeal for the oat flour for a very different texture.

If you prefer to use honey instead of brown sugar, use only 1½ tablespoons and add it to the liquid ingredients instead of the dry. (If you measure the oil first, the honey won't stick to the tablespoon.)

BISCUITS

Biscuit batter is very forgiving—unless you handle it too much. Then you'll have silver-dollar-sized biscuits on your hands.

You can combine unbleached, all-purpose flour with smaller quantities of other flour types. Try substituting barley flour for ⅓ of the unbleached, all-purpose flour. Rye flour is a nice strong substitute.

As for the fat in the recipe, butter, shortening, or oil can be used. Of the three, it's probably easiest to use vegetable oil. Safflower oil is a flavorless oil I've used with much success. Shortening, which is hydrogenated vegetable fat, is inexpensive and also flavorless. It can be worked into the dough with a pastry blender or two knives, which minimizes handling. Butter will produce a good biscuit, but why not use the cheaper oil as an ingredient and save your butter for melting over the freshly baked biscuit?

Basic Baking Powder Biscuits

Leftover biscuits can become dry pretty quickly, so use them in a manner that disguises this. For example, slice the biscuits in half, top them with a cream sauce to which flaked fish has been added, and bake them for 15 minutes at 325° F. The biscuits will remoisten and taste as good as fresh. Plain biscuits can be refreshed by wrapping them in a moist (not wet!) cloth and placing them inside a pan with a lid in a 350° F. oven for about 5 minutes. Watch this procedure carefully or the cloth will burn.

If kept in an airtight container, biscuits will stay fresh for two or three days at room temperature. I use them to make mini-open-faced sandwiches to accompany soup.

Use a sharp cookie cutter or knife to cut out biscuits. There's no point in keeping the dough nice and light if you mash it down with a dull-lipped glass.

1 cup unbleached, all-purpose flour
2 teaspoons baking powder
pinch salt
2 tablespoons vegetable oil
⅓ cup milk

Preheat the oven to 425° F.

Combine the dry ingredients in a mixing bowl. Quickly and lightly mix in the oil until it is evenly distributed. Then add the milk and stir until the dough is moist and sticky throughout. This should take only a moment or two of stirring.

Flour your breadboard and turn the biscuit dough onto it. Then gently sprinkle the dough with a light coating of flour and knead it about 10 times, flouring lightly in the places where it sticks. Roll to a ½-inch thickness and cut into biscuits with a sharp cookie cutter. Bake on an ungreased cookie sheet for 15 minutes.

Variations

- If you increase the milk to ½ cup, you will have drop biscuits. Drop them by the spoonful onto an ungreased cookie sheet and proceed.
- Toss a tablespoon of grated cheddar cheese into the flour mixture, and allow the flour to coat the cheese before adding the oil and milk.
- Add 2 teaspoons of grated Parmesan or Romano cheese to the flour.
- Mix 2 tablespoons of yogurt into the moist ingredients.
- Toss in a teaspoon of dill weed.
- Fennel and coriander are both very good in biscuits. Try about ¼ teaspoon crushed fennel seed or ⅛ teaspoon ground coriander.
- For a sweeter result, a teaspoon of allspice or cinnamon is good, especially if honey is drizzled on the biscuits once they're cooked.

QUICKBREAD LOAVES

These recipes are ideal for one person. They are designed to produce one mini-loaf (6"x3¼"x2"), so leftovers are never a problem. While the breads are on the sweet side, they are also versatile and are easily matched with a selection of cheeses and nut butters as luncheon fare. For dessert, heat a slice and top with a berry sauce (p. 175).

The bread will keep for up to three weeks in the refrigerator if wrapped securely in plastic wrap. Before freezing a loaf, slice it to assure efficient use in the future; freeze the slices separately.

Mixing the batter for quickbread loaves is similar in technique to the preparation of muffins. To avoid overbeating, the dry ingredients are mixed in one bowl, the egg mixture in another. The two halves are then combined and mixed at the last moment, just until evenly blended.

If you don't have a mini-loaf pan, any baking dish with vertical sides and a 2-cup capacity will work just as well.

Poppy Seed Bread

1 MINI-LOAF

The poppy seeds are abundant in this recipe and they provide a wonderful texture. They keep indefinitely, so you can make this bread any time.

⅔ cup unbleached, all-purpose flour
1 teaspoon baking powder
1 egg
3 tablespoons granulated sugar
3 tablespoons vegetable oil
⅓ cup half-and-half
¼ teaspoon vanilla
¼ cup poppy seeds

Preheat the oven to 350° F.

Grease and flour a mini-loaf pan (6"x3¼"x2"). Combine the flour and the baking powder. In a separate bowl, beat the egg slightly and mix with the sugar. Add the oil, half-and-half, and vanilla and stir until well mixed.

Pour the egg mixture into the flour mixture, add the poppy seeds, and stir until evenly distributed. Turn the batter into the mini-loaf pan and bake for 45 to 50 minutes, or until a knife inserted into the center of the loaf comes out clean. Remove from the pan and cool on a rack.

Middle Eastern Pumpkin Bread

I love the way pumpkin responds to cumin and turmeric, so to me, putting curry powder in a pumpkin bread is a logical development. The result is a versatile and tasty loaf. When thinly sliced and spread with cream cheese, it makes a good sandwich. Also, you may heat it in the oven and eat it like cake, topped with whipped cream.

1 cup unbleached, all-purpose flour
½ teaspoon baking soda
¼ teaspoon salt
1 teaspoon curry powder
1 egg, slightly beaten
½ cup brown sugar
½ cup cooked, mashed pumpkin
2 tablespoons water
¼ cup butter, softened
½ cup chopped walnuts or pecans

Preheat the oven to 350° F.
Grease and flour a mini-loaf pan (6"x3¼"x2") or a straight-sided baking dish of 2-cup capacity.

Mix the flour, baking soda, salt, and curry powder. In a separate bowl, combine the beaten egg with the brown sugar, then add the pumpkin, water, and soft butter. Pour the liquid ingredients into the flour mixture, add the nuts, and stir until well mixed.

Pour the batter into the greased and floured loaf pan and bake for 50–60 minutes, or until a knife inserted into the center of the loaf comes out clean. Remove from the pan and cool on a rack.

Banana Bread

This is a very tidy recipe. It uses one ripe banana and makes one mini-loaf. The result is moist and fragrant—a nice return for very little effort.

2 tablespoons butter, softened
2 tablespoons brown sugar
1 ripe banana, mashed and strained
  through a sieve
1 egg, slightly beaten
1 teaspoon lemon juice
⅛ teaspoon allspice or nutmeg
¼ cup chopped pecans or walnuts
pinch salt
½ teaspoon baking powder
¾ cup unbleached, all-purpose flour

Preheat the oven to 350° F.
Grease and flour a mini-loaf pan.

Cream together the butter and sugar. Add the banana, egg, juice, and spice, and beat 35–40 times with a wooden spoon. Add the nuts and stir to mix. Add the salt and baking powder to the flour. Sprinkle the flour mixture into the batter and stir until thoroughly combined. Pour the batter into the pan and bake for 50–60 minutes or until a knife inserted into the center of the loaf comes out clean. Remove from the pan and cool on a rack.

Zucchini Bread

This little loaf gets many good things from the zucchini—its light, sweet flavor, its hearty texture, and its moisture.

2 tablespoons raisins
½ cup unbleached, all-purpose flour
½ teaspoon allspice
¼ teaspoon salt
½ teaspoon baking soda
¼ teaspoon baking powder
1 egg
3 tablespoons granulated sugar
3 tablespoons vegetable oil
½ cup grated zucchini
⅓ cup chopped walnuts

Preheat the oven to 350° F.

Plump the raisins by covering them in warm water for 15–20 minutes. Grease and flour a mini-loaf pan (6"x3¼"x2") or any vertical-sided baking dish with a 2-cup capacity.

Sift together all the dry ingredients except the granulated sugar. In a separate bowl, beat the egg slightly, and mix with the sugar. Add the oil, grated zucchini, walnuts, and drained raisins. Pour the liquid ingredients into the flour mixture and stir until just mixed.

Pour the batter into the mini-loaf pan and bake for 50 minutes, or until a knife inserted into the center of the loaf comes out clean. Remove the bread from the pan and cool on a rack.

Basic Stuffing

Stuffing is one of the most creative "starches" you can put on your menu. You can gauge the quantity to make by estimating how many pieces of bread you could eat in its place. This recipe is only one idea. It should be made from stale bread or bread heels—the drier, the better.

1 celery rib, diced
¼ apple, chopped
2 tablespoons chopped onion
3–4 mushrooms, sliced
2 tablespoons butter
2 bread slices, broken into bite-sized
   pieces
2 tablespoons chopped walnuts
⅓ cup chicken stock (p. 21)
2 teaspoons sage
¼ teaspoon celery salt

Preheat the oven to 350° F.

Sauté the celery, apple, onion, and mushrooms in the butter. Add the bread pieces and the remaining ingredients. Toss to distribute the moisture.

Bake in a greased, covered dish for 30 minutes, or loosely stuff into the cavity of a Cornish hen (p. 116).

Flexi Wheat Bread

This is a basic wheat bread which can become the bread of your choice when you substitute different ingredients. See the suggested substitutes.

> ### ⇒ SEEDS ⇐
>
> For best results, choose only one and add only the indicated amount.
>
> | | |
> |---|---|
> | Sesame seed | 1 tablespoon |
> | Caraway seed | 1 teaspoon |
> | Cumin seed, lightly crushed | ½ teaspoon |
> | Anise seed (star anise), lightly crushed | ¼ teaspoon |
> | Fennel seed, lightly crushed | ½ teaspoon |

1½ tablespoons vegetable oil, margarine, or butter
1 tablespoon honey
¾ cup HOT tap water
1 tablespoon granular yeast (1¼-ounce package dry yeast)
¾ cup whole wheat flour
½ cup flour of your choice (see p. 65)
¼ teaspoon salt
¼ cup embellishments (see p. 66)
seeds, herbs, or spices (see pp. 64-66)

In a medium-sized mixing bowl, combine the oil, honey, and HOT tap water. Stir to dissolve the honey. When the water has cooled to lukewarm, sprinkle the yeast over it, stir to moisten, then let it sit for 5 minutes to proof.

In a large mixing bowl, combine ½ cup whole wheat flour, ¼ cup of the flour of your choice, and ¼ teaspoon salt. Once the yeast has proofed, add the liquid mixture to the flour mixture and stir vigorously with a wooden spoon for 200 strokes. The batter will become cohesive, and the spoon will leave a sticky trail in the batter.

If desired, set the dough to rise for an hour, until it has doubled in bulk. Allowing the dough to rise at this stage will produce a lighter, more tender loaf.

The next step is to add the remaining ¼ cup whole wheat flour and ¼ cup flour of your choice, the embellishments, and the seeds, herbs, or spices.

Work the flour mixture into the dough by pressing from the outside of the ball into the center, turning the bowl as you go. As the dough becomes more unified, begin kneading it. Knead with a folding and pushing motion for a solid 10 minutes. Sprinkle with flour as needed.

Set the dough to rise in a mixing bowl that has been very lightly oiled. You can use the same bowl you used for mixing. When you place the ball of dough in the bowl, gently roll it around to coat it lightly with oil as well. Cover with a moist, clean towel and set in a warm, draft-free spot until the dough has doubled in bulk.

Once doubled, punch the dough down with your fists and work it briefly until the dough is smooth and free of large air bubbles. If you are going to make two loaves, cut the dough in half now.

Grease and flour the loaf pans. Form the loaves and set them to rise in the loaf pans until the dough forms a dome over the top of the pan. Midway through this rise (about 15 minutes) you will need to preheat the oven to 350° F. Bake the risen loaves for 40 to 55 minutes (40 minutes for the mini-loaves, 55 minutes for a standard loaf).

Remove the bread from the pan as soon as it has baked, and set it to cool on a rack. If a softer crust is desired, spread the top of the loaf with butter or cover the loaf with a clean, dry towel as it cools.

⇒ HONEY SUBSTITUTES ⇐

Instead of 1 tablespoon honey, add:

Granulated sugar	1 teaspoon
Brown sugar	1 teaspoon
Molasses	1 tablespoon
Maple syrup	1 tablespoon

⇒ FLOUR SUBSTITUTES ⇐

Up to ½ cup of the following flours may be used unless otherwise indicated. If less than ½ cup is used, the difference must be made up with whole wheat flour or unbleached, all-purpose flour.

Unbleached, all-purpose flour	½ cup will produce a lighter loaf, or you may make the loaf entirely out of unbleached, all-purpose flour.
Rye flour or buckwheat flour	½ cup of one of these flours will produce a heavier loaf.
Soy flour	Mix ¼ cup with ¼ cup of unbleached, all-purpose flour.
Oat flour	Make your own oat flour by whirling dry oatmeal in a blender. I recommend using ½ cup and sweetening the loaf with molasses (see Honey Substitutes, p. 65).
Cooked cereal	Add up to ½ cup of leftover oatmeal, mixed grain cereal, cream of wheat, etc.
Cornmeal	Mix ¼ cup with ¼ cup unbleached, all-purpose flour.

⇒ HERBS ⇐

Choose one of the following.

Dill weed	1 teaspoon fresh, or ½ teaspoon dried
Rosemary	1 teaspoon fresh, or ½ teaspoon dried
Marjoram	1 teaspoon fresh, or ½ teaspoon dried
Sage	1 teaspoon fresh, or ½ teaspoon dried
Chives	Use up to 2 teaspoons chopped fresh chives, in addition to other herbs.

⇒SPICES⇐

Use ¼ teaspoon of the following spices. Choose only one, or experiment with a combination of spices that does not total more than ¼ teaspoon when combined. Exceptions to this are indicated below.

Allspice	¼ teaspoon
Cinnamon	¼ teaspoon
Nutmeg	¼ teaspoon
Mace	¼ teaspoon
Ginger	¼ teaspoon
Cardamom	⅛ teaspoon
Pepper	⅛ teaspoon is good with rosemary, sage, or grated Parmesan cheese.
Curry powder	1 teaspoon
Coriander	1 teaspoon may be used along with the specified amount of curry powder, allspice, or cardamom.

⇒EMBELLISHMENTS⇐

Add up to ¼ cup of the following ingredients unless otherwise noted. Some of the ingredients can be added in combination with others as indicated. You needn't limit yourself to one choice.

Wheat germ	2 tablespoons
Nonfat dry milk solids	¼ cup
Chopped nuts	¼ cup may be added in addition to other embellishment choices.
Plumped raisins or currants	¼ cup may be added in addition to other embellishment choices.
Sautéed chopped onion	¼ cup may be added in addition to other embellishment choices. Onions are good with grated Parmesan cheese or mashed potatoes, and they combine well with many different herbs and spices.
Parmesan cheese	¼ cup
Mashed potatoes	3 tablespoons may be added in addition to other embellishment choices.
Granola	¼ cup adds excellent texture. Combine with cinnamon, nutmeg, or allspice, and perhaps some raisins.

VEGETABLES

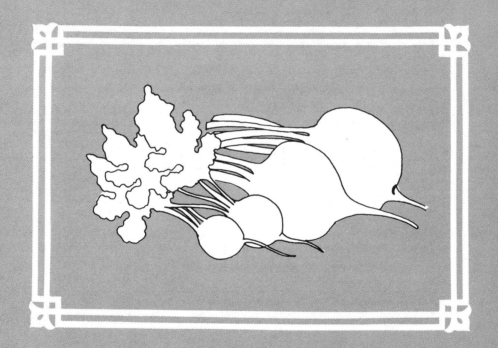

It's easy for me to use fresh produce frequently since the San Francisco Bay area has such a bountiful supply the year round. I realize that some of you are not as fortunate. When possible, however, I urge you to make good use of fresh produce, both for the nutrients and for the satisfaction of preparing it well. Trimming greens for a salad, scrubbing carrots, or slicing zucchini with a good sharp knife can provide great pleasure.

On the other hand, a surplus of produce can become a burden if it is on the verge of spoiling. The best way to salvage the situation is to freeze the vegetables for future use, even though the freezing and subsequent reheating will result in some nutrient loss. To increase the likelihood that you'll eat them later, vegetables should be frozen in a form that is as ready-to-eat as possible.

Have a pot of boiling water ready. Trim the vegetables as for cooking. Place them in the boiling water and cover. Cook only to heat through—3 minutes by the clock. This is called blanching. Fill another saucepan or mixing bowl with cold water. When the vegetables have completed the 3 minutes of heating, drain them immediately and put them in the cold water for an additional 3 minutes. Drain thoroughly, then blot dry with towelling. Freeze in freezer bags in quantities suitable for future portions. Tie the bag with string, allowing ½ inch of space at the top of the vegetables.

Don't thaw the frozen vegetables before cooking. Place them in about ½ inch boiling water and cover until tender—from 5 to 10 minutes depending on the size and density of the pieces.

An effective way to limit spoilage of fresh produce is to keep your crisper dry and clean. Remove most of the greens from radishes, carrots, beets, and the like before putting them away. Trim the roots from green onions before storing, also. Store each type of produce separately in a loose, open plastic bag.

Fresh vegetables, as a general rule, *must not* be overcooked. When done correctly, you will need to bite and chew, yet the vegetable won't crunch. This perfect state is called "al dente" in honor of the teeth we use all too seldom.

SALADS

If a food can be cut into bite-sized pieces, it can go into a tossed green salad. Typically, though, a tossed green salad is a medley of vegetables, beans, nuts, and seeds. If you do fresh food shopping on a weekly basis, you should always have enough ingredients on hand for a salad.

Crumbled or diced cheese is delicious with a good strong lettuce or green. Cheddar cubes, crumbled feta, and strips of Swiss are examples. Use nuts such as chopped walnuts, pecans, peanuts, and almonds; and seeds like sesame, sunflower, and pumpkin seeds. Use the untreated, unsalted varieties worthy of your other salad ingredients.

Salads are perhaps the best way to use leftovers, because the leftovers don't have to be reheated, and therefore fewer nutrients are lost. And leftovers are not restricted to vegetables by any means! Cold poultry, meat, and fish give a salad the nutritional substance of a main dish, as do hard-cooked eggs.

As soon as you put dressing on a salad, it begins to wilt dramatically. Also, lettuce will begin to wilt as soon as it is exposed to the juice from cut tomatoes or fruit. It is, therefore, not economical to make salad portions larger than you intend to eat right away. To avoid potential waste, first chop the salad ingredients, dressing them with salt, pepper, and fresh or dried herbs. Next, tear in only the amount of lettuce needed for one serving, and, finally, lightly dress the leaves with a good salad oil, preferably olive oil, and a smaller amount of lemon juice or vinegar. It is contrary to the spirit of a tossed green salad to mask the flavors of the featured ingredients. They should be enhanced, and a lemon juice or vinegar and oil dressing achieves this very nicely. Three parts oil to one part vinegar or lemon juice is a standard ratio, although the oil can be cut way back with good results.

Spinach Salad I
1 MAIN-DISH SALAD

The cheddar cheese gives this salad the substance of a light main dish; it is delicious with hot rolls or bread. It is also a good companion to a cream soup or chowder.

1½ cups spinach, torn into bite-sized pieces and loosely packed
¼ cup diced cheddar cheese
¼ cup sliced mushrooms
2 tablespoons chopped green onion (1 green onion)
1 small beet, diced

Assemble the ingredients in a medium-sized bowl, and top with a vinaigrette dressing. Toss gently to coat the leaves.

Spinach Salad II
1–2 PORTIONS

Tangy citrus gives this spinach salad a completely different dimension. If you don't have grapefruit on hand, try using an orange instead.

1½–2 cups spinach, torn into bite-sized pieces and loosely packed
½ avocado, sliced
½ grapefruit, peeled, membrane removed, cut into bite-sized pieces
3 tablespoons chopped pecans or walnuts
4 *thin* Bermuda onion slices

Combine all the ingredients in a salad bowl, top with a vinaigrette dressing, and toss gently to coat the spinach.

Rabbit Salad

This salad is a riot of color and has a wonderful crisp, crunchy texture. It makes a great companion to a creamy frittata or a pasta entrée. Serve it nested in a red cabbage leaf. Most of these ingredients are available any time of year.

¼ cup thinly sliced and chopped red cabbage
½ carrot, cut into small dice
3 tablespoons chopped green pepper
1 medium-sized tomato, chopped
¼ cup chopped celery, including leaves
1 green onion, finely chopped
pinch salt
pinch pepper
¼ teaspoon celery salt
3 tablespoons tomato juice or tomato-based vegetable juice
1 tablespoon vinegar
2 tablespoons olive oil

Assemble all the vegetables in a salad bowl. Combine the remaining ingredients. Pour the dressing over the salad, toss gently, and serve.

Yogurt Fruit Salad

If you add ripe fruit to plain yogurt and allow it to marinate overnight, you'll be surprised at how sweet it is without the addition of honey.

Leftover yogurt salad will keep for three days in a covered container in the refrigerator.

1½ tablespoons marmalade
1½ tablespoons apple butter
½ apple, sliced (honey, optional)
½ peach, sliced (honey, optional)
⅛ cantaloupe, diced
½ papaya, diced
¼ cup toasted wheat germ
¼ cup applesauce
1 mashed banana
sprinkling of chopped nuts

Mix ½ cup plain yogurt with one or more of the ingredients.

Horiatiki

This Greek main-dish salad is at its best when the tomatoes are vine-ripened, sweet, and vivid. A good alternative to the mealy, anemic fare usually available in supermarkets is cherry tomatoes, cut in half. Feta cheese, packed in brine, is sold in 8- or 16-ounce containers in delis, cheese shops, or Greek specialty stores. Feta cheese keeps for several weeks when stored in its own brine in a sealed container in the refrigerator.

1 large tomato, cut into wedges, or 8–10 cherry tomatoes, cut in half
¼ Bermuda onion, thinly sliced into rings
8–10 Greek olives
2 teaspoons olive oil
1½ tablespoons lemon juice
¼ teaspoon oregano
⅛ teaspoon dill weed
¼ cup feta cheese

In a medium-sized bowl, combine everything but the feta cheese. Once the tomato is coated with the juice and oil, crumble the feta cheese on top. Serve.

Mediterranean Orange Salad

The oranges are marinated in a spiced vinaigrette to give an interesting aspect to this cool and juicy fruit. Orange Salad makes a good accompaniment to Stuffed Eggplant (p. 91).

2 teaspoons olive oil
1 tablespoon vinegar
½ teaspoon coriander
⅛ teaspoon dry mustard
pinch pepper
1 orange, peeled and thinly sliced
lettuce
⅛ teaspoon dried mint, optional

In a small bowl combine everything but the orange slices, lettuce, and mint. Arrange the orange slices on a bed of lettuce on a salad plate and cover with the dressing. Garnish with mint if desired.

Variation

Combine the orange slices with thin slices of Bermuda onion, crumbled bleu cheese, and romaine lettuce. Dress with salt, pepper, and a vinaigrette dressing.

Peanut Rice Salad

This delicious salad is really just a quick chopping and assembly job. If you want to create a tour de force, spend a few extra minutes making Peanut Butter Dressing, p. 180.

Leftover rice salad will keep for three days in a covered container in the refrigerator.

1 cup cooked long-grain brown rice
¼ cup raisins, plumped in warm water for 15–20 minutes
¼ cup shelled and halved peanuts (unsalted)
1 green onion, thinly sliced
¼ cup diced celery
½ small apple, chopped into small dice
2 teaspoons coriander
⅛ teaspoon salt
pinch pepper

Place all the ingredients in a medium-sized salad bowl and toss gently to mix.

Cold Pasta Salad I

Any pasta will do, but if you are using lasagna noodles or large pasta shells, cut them into bite-sized pieces before mixing with the other ingredients.

Leftover salad will keep for four days in a covered container in the refrigerator.

1 cup cold cooked pasta
2 ounces sardines or herring
⅓ cup cooked peas
1 tablespoon minced onion
⅛ teaspoon celery seed
¼ teaspoon oregano
salt to taste
⅛ teaspoon pepper
2 tablespoons mayonnaise

In a medium-sized mixing bowl, combine all but the mayonnaise. Then add the mayonnaise, stir gently, and serve.

Cold Pasta Salad II

This pasta salad has an Italian flavor. Oil, garlic, tomato, and fennel suggest a cold version of spaghetti with tomato sauce. The result, however, is quite different and delightful.

Leftover salad will keep for four days in a covered container in the refrigerator.

2 tablespoons olive oil
1 garlic clove, crushed
1 tablespoon vinegar
⅛ teaspoon fennel seed, crushed
1 cup cold cooked pasta
8 capers
1 medium-sized tomato, chopped
6–8 black olives
2 tablespoons chopped fresh
  parsley
pinch salt
pinch pepper

Combine the oil, garlic, vinegar, and fennel seed. In a medium-sized bowl, combine the remaining ingredients. Dress with the oil mixture and toss lightly to coat.

Raita

This Indian yogurt salad is the ideal cool, fresh foil to a spicy entrée. In this raita, a recommended ingredient is fresh cilantro leaves, available in Indian, Mexican, or Chinese produce markets, and sometimes in the supermarket. Fresh parsley can be substituted in the absence of cilantro.

½ cup plain yogurt
1 tablespoon torn fresh cilantro
  leaves, or fresh parsley
1 small tomato, diced
¼ cup thinly sliced, quartered, and
  peeled cucumber
2 teaspoons coriander

Assemble the ingredients and allow them to marinate overnight if possible, or at least for an hour.

Artichoke with Dip

An artichoke is meant to be eaten lingeringly. That's why it grows the way it does. It's what I call a social or contemplative vegetable—the perfect choice for a meal when you're reading a book that you just can't put down. Save the artichoke bottom to make Cream of Artichoke Soup, p.23.

8 cups water
2–4 teaspoons lemon juice
2 tablespoons olive oil
1 artichoke, trimmed as shown

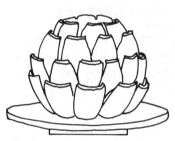

Bring the water, lemon juice, and oil to a boil. Then add the artichoke and cook in a gently rolling boil for 40 minutes.

Serve the artichoke accompanied by a dip of mayonnaise seasoned with dill, lemon, chives, or curry. Also melted butter, lemon butter, sour cream, or yogurt makes a delicious dip.

Artichoke Heart Stew

This meatless recipe is a delicate mélange of vegetables heated in a light and clear lemon sauce which is virtually fat-free. The artichoke hearts are not marinated. They can be obtained in frozen 9-ounce boxes, or jars of varying sizes (about 14–16 ounces). A quick side dish to accompany this meal is pasta tossed with grated Parmesan cheese and fresh parsley.

4 small boiling onions
⅔ cup chicken stock (p. 21)
1½ tablespoons cornstarch
1½ tablespoons cold water
1 tablespoon plus 2 teaspoons lemon juice
1 teaspoon dill weed
pinch celery salt
7–9 small mushroom caps
1 cup artichoke hearts

Begin by peeling the onions and boiling them in a saucepan with water to cover until they are tender. This will take about 8 minutes.

In another saucepan bring the chicken stock to a boil. Make a paste of the cornstarch and water. Add the smooth (lump-free) cornstarch and water mixture to the chicken stock and stir until the sauce thickens, about 5 minutes. Add the lemon juice, dill weed, and celery salt, and stir. Then add the mushroom caps, onions, and artichoke hearts, and cover. Reduce the heat and allow the mixture to simmer for about 10 minutes or until heated through. Serve.

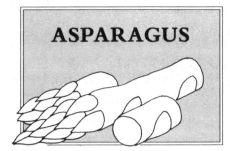

ASPARAGUS

Asparagus is precious stuff! It's not easy to get fresh and when it is available, it costs. It's easy to overcook, you can't eat it raw, and if you keep it around too long, it goes limp on you. That doesn't seem to stop us, though. Many of us could eat an asparagus omelet for breakfast, have cream of asparagus soup for lunch, down a few cold spears with mayo as a snack, and finish the day with stir-fry chicken and asparagus for dinner.

As far as purists are concerned, steamed is the only way to go. Gently rinse as many spears as you intend to steam. Grasp the **bottom of each spear with one hand, and with your other hand guide the spear to snap off as close to the bottom as possible.**

Place the raw spears in ½ inch boiling water, or in a steamer over the water. Cover and allow to cook for about 4 minutes. Check for doneness each ½ minute thereafter. When done, spears should be only slightly softened and still vividly green.

If the asparagus is done before you are ready to serve, remove the asparagus from the boiling water. Keep the water in the pan and turn off the burner for now. Shock the asparagus by submerging it in cold water for about 10 seconds, and place it on a covered platter until you are almost ready to serve. Then turn on the burner and immerse the asparagus for about 30 seconds, just to get it hot.

Hot asparagus is a natural for lemon butter, fresh ground pepper, and a tiny bit of salt. Also, a fresh squeeze of lemon and plain butter is excellent. Along with the butter, try some dill weed, or a combination of crushed Italian herbs including oregano, basil, and thyme. Finally, asparagus with Hollandaise Sauce (p. 178) is one cliché worth repeating.

Asparagus can be quickly chilled by allowing it to stand in cold water for 5 minutes or so. Don't run it under cold water, since it is delicate once cooked and can bruise easily. If you are cooking asparagus especially to be eaten cold, cook it less, rather than more. It holds its color and shape much more nicely. When softer, asparagus can become stringy.

Cold asparagus spears can be worked into an imaginative julienne vegetable salad. A dressing with a hint of horseradish is tasty and dramatic with asparagus. Of course, a simple vinaigrette with your choice of ground herbs is always good.

For more ideas, try one of these:

- cream of asparagus soup
- asparagus in a green salad
- asparagus in an omelet or frittata
- crêpes stuffed with asparagus and topped with a cream sauce
- asparagus quiche
- asparagus soufflé

Asparagus Mornay

This is a quick meal, but you have to work for it. In the order given, you'll be hard-cooking an egg, making Sauce Mornay, steaming asparagus, and then broiling the assembled dish. (The egg may be cooked in advance, but it will be desirable to have it at least at room temperature. If it is stone cold, even the broiler may not warm it through in 1 minute.)

4–5 asparagus spears
1 egg, hard-cooked and sliced
½ cup Sauce Mornay (p. 182)

Turn on the broiler, and steam 4–5 asparagus spears on top of the stove (see p. 77). Place the asparagus spears in a ramekin with about 1½-cup capacity, cover with the sliced egg, then add the sauce. Place the assembled dish under the broiler for about 1 minute, or until the sauce bubbles. Serve.

Guacamole

The trick here is to keep the guacamole from getting brown—the lemon juice acts as an antioxidant. Keep guacamole covered once made and don't make it too far in advance.

Guacamole makes a great dip for tortilla chips and all kinds of raw vegetables. Try it as a filling for sandwiches, burritos, tacos, and pita bread, and as a topping for bean casseroles or tostadas.

½ avocado
2 teaspoons lemon juice
dash Tabasco sauce
1 green onion, minced
2 tablespoons sour cream or yogurt
pinch cayenne
pinch salt
pinch pepper
1 garlic clove, crushed, optional

Mash the avocado with the lemon juice in a bowl, then add the rest of the ingredients. Serve at once or store in a covered container in the refrigerator for up to two days.

Shrimp-Stuffed Avocado

The avocado is a marvelous oil-rich fruit that will always seem exotic to me—even though I lived in southern California for several years.

⅓ cup cooked shrimp
1 teaspoon dill weed
2 tablespoons mayonnaise
pinch salt
pinch pepper
1 teaspoon vinegar
½ avocado

Combine the first six ingredients and spoon into half of a peeled, pitted, ripe avocado.

FRESH GREEN BEANS

Green beans are best when firm, taut, green, and with the tiniest bit of silvery fuzz. When preparing for cooking, wash only those beans you intend to eat. String the larger beans when necessary by breaking off the stem end and pulling lengthwise.

Serving Suggestions

Try the beans in some of the following ways:

- with sautéed onions
- with slivered almonds
- with chopped nuts
- as a bed for a poached egg
- as a companion to a broiled tomato
- julienne, with mushroom slices
- cold, with mayonnaise

Swiss Green Beans

1–2 PORTIONS

I consider this recipe to be tasty and varied enough to be a light one-dish meal, but a full supper could include a piece of baked chicken. Select a pan with a lid that is suitable for both stovetop and oven.

1 dozen fresh green beans (1½ cups cooked)
2 tablespoons chopped onion
1 tablespoon olive oil
1 tablespoon whole wheat flour
⅛ teaspoon salt
pinch pepper
½ teaspoon grated lemon peel
1 tablespoon fresh parsley, chopped
2 tablespoons sour cream
2 tablespoons grated sharp cheddar cheese
1 tablespoon butter, melted
¼ cup breadcrumbs

Preheat the oven to 350° F.

Steam the beans until they are just tender, then shock them by dunking them briefly in cold water to stop them from cooking. Set them aside. Sauté the onion in the olive oil until it is translucent. Add the flour, salt, pepper, lemon peel, parsley, and sour cream. Stir to mix, and then heat through. Return the green beans to the pan and toss with the sour cream mixture. Sprinkle the cheese over the green beans.

Make a mixture of the melted butter and breadcrumbs and sprinkle over the beans. Place in the oven and bake for 20 minutes. Serve hot.

Sweet and Sour Beets

My mom makes something similar to this called Harvard Beets. If you're cooking the beet yourself, save the liquid from the beet and use it in this recipe.

Leftover Sweet and Sour Beets can be kept in a covered container in the refrigerator for four days.

2 teaspoons cornstarch
2 teaspoons cold water
1 tablespoon honey
pinch salt
1 whole clove
2 tablespoons lemon juice
1 teaspoon grated lemon peel
¾ cup beet cooking liquid or water
1 cooked beet, sliced

Dissolve the cornstarch in 2 teaspoons cold water. Then combine all the ingredients except the sliced beet in a heavy saucepan or double boiler. Stirring constantly, cook the mixture until it thickens and is no longer cloudy. Remove the clove. Add the beet slices, heat through, and serve.

Pickled Beets

As the name implies, this method of preparation allows you to keep the beet for a longer time—about three weeks. You will need a cooked beet, and I suggest slicing it into sticks of chopstick or pencil thickness for easy storage in a jar.

½ cup vinegar
1½ cups water
2 whole cloves
pinch salt
pinch pepper, or 3–4 peppercorns
1 teaspoon honey
2 tablespoons chopped onion
2 tablespoons chopped green pepper
2–3 whole, dried allspice berries, optional
1 cooked beet, sliced

Boil everything but the beet to permit dissolving and blending of flavors. Allow the mixture to cool slightly, and then combine it with the beet in a jar. Keep refrigerated until ready to use.

BROCCOLI

This vegetable is plentiful almost year-round here in San Francisco. The only drawback I find is the size of the bunches. To offset this minor problem, remember that fresh broccoli keeps quite well for up to a week, and steamed-and-shocked broccoli freezes nicely for long-term storage. If you have part or all of a broccoli bunch that is on the verge of wilting, act quickly!

Freezing. Cut the broccoli into chunks and steam it until it is not quite tender. Then soak it for an equal amount of time in cold water. This technique prepares the broccoli for freezing once it has cooled. Drain the broccoli and blot it dry before placing it in a freezer container. Label the freezing bag or container with the contents and the date. Use within three months.

Leftovers. Cooked broccoli can be used in a wide variety of ways. It's best not to reheat it for the most nutritional value, but once in a while won't hurt. For example:
- Make a Broccoli Frittata (p. 15).
- Purée into a cream soup.
- Serve cold with tomato wedges and a vinaigrette dressing.
- Reheat with leftover mashed potatoes and a boiled sausage.

Broccoli Supreme

1 MAIN–DISH PORTION

If you make the rice in a pan that can go in the oven, you'll be saving yourself a dishwashing step. Vary the cheese when you make it the second time. Cheddar and walnuts produce a very different result.

You'll need to allow 40 minutes for the rice to cook if you haven't any leftovers on hand.

¼ cup long-grain brown rice, cooked
½ cup broccoli florets
4 large mushrooms, sliced
⅓ cup grated Swiss cheese
1 tablespoon butter
1 tablespoon lemon juice

Preheat the oven to 350° F.

Place the cooked rice in the bottom of an individual casserole dish and add the broccoli, mushrooms, and cheese. Top with butter and lemon and bake for 25–30 minutes. The broccoli should be al dente when done.

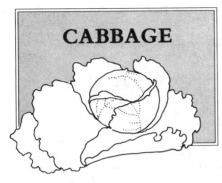

CABBAGE

There are many possibilities for preparing cabbage, either raw or cooked. Raw cabbage can be shredded into any number of slaws, or the whole leaf can be used to cradle cold salads. Cabbage can be steamed plain with butter or put into soups, or used as a casing for stuffed cabbage.

One reason cabbage makes such a good buy is that it keeps so well. Nutrients are reduced after two weeks, but it can be kept for up to a month with good cooking results.

Sweet and Sour Cabbage

1–2 PORTIONS

This dish can be eaten chilled, too. If you have any leftovers, they'll keep for a good week in the refrigerator. If you can take the time to bring the cold salad to room temperature, you'll notice that the flavors are nicely enhanced through just that bit of warming. Just set the dish on the counter about an hour before you're ready to eat.

3 onion slices
1 tablespoon olive oil
½ cup shredded cabbage
1½ teaspoons vinegar
2 tablespoons water
1 tablespoon red wine, optional
pinch salt
pinch pepper
1 apple, cored and unpeeled, sliced
½ teaspoon honey

Sauté the onion in the hot olive oil. Add everything else but the honey and cook over low heat until the cabbage and apple are tender. Stir the honey into the mixture once cooking is complete, then serve.

Steamed Cabbage Dijon

1 PORTION

This quick-cooking dish is buttery, crisp, and tangy. Prepare it with a German menu—bockwurst and warm applesauce.

5–6 thin wedges of cabbage
1 tablespoon butter, softened
½ teaspoon Dijon or other prepared mustard

Steam the cabbage wedges over boiling water for 5 minutes. While the cabbage steams, combine the mustard and butter. Once the cabbage has completed cooking, toss it with the mustard mixture, and serve.

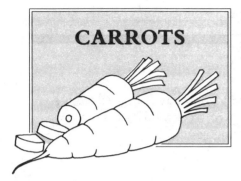

CARROTS

You don't want to peel carrots, since there are so many nutrients in and under the skin. Just run the carrot under cold water and scrape the skin free of any dirty spots, using a vegetable brush.

Grating raw carrots is a wonderful way to enhance the texture and nutrient value of many, many salads and main dishes. Use this method also to get rid of aging carrots or to brighten a meal. Try one of the following ideas:

- Add to thick bean soup or hearty vegetable soup.
- Add up to ½ cup to main-dish grain loaves for added moisture, texture, and color.
- Add up to ¼ cup to a quickbread batter.
- Steam for about 4 minutes for a quick side dish. Try adding an equal amount of grated zucchini after the first 2 minutes of steaming. Toss with grated cheddar cheese, chopped nuts, butter, and/or lemon juice.
- Bake in a casserole: Oil the casserole dish and place in it 3 parts grated carrot to 1 part milk. Season with about ⅛ teaspoon

☙GRATED CARROT SALAD❧

Grate a couple of raw carrots and add to them a few choices from the following list.

Dress the salad with 1 teaspoon honey, 2 teaspoons vinegar, and 2 teaspoons vegetable oil.

Leftover carrot salad will keep for up to a week in a covered container in the refrigerator. If the salad is dressed, however, or if you have added zucchini, you'll want to use leftovers within two or three days.

- ¼ cup raisins, plumped
- 2 tablespoons sunflower seeds
- ¼ cup chopped pineapple
- 2 tablespoons chopped walnuts or cashews
- ⅓ cup grated zucchini

ginger for each ½ cup of carrots. Top with 2 teaspoons butter. Bake at 350° F. for 25 minutes.

Cooked Carrots

If you don't like cooked carrots, perhaps it's because you've only eaten them plain. With very little trouble they can be enhanced with spices, cream, or other vegetables. Once cooked, the carrots can be sautéed lightly in butter, bathed in dill weed, and immersed in cream, which is then reduced over high heat to make a thick sauce.

Mashing cooked carrots is another way to allow the natural sweetness to emerge. Mash cooked carrots with a potato masher or rice them by forcing them through a food mill. Add broth, water, or milk to achieve the desired consistency, then add butter and season with ⅛ teaspoon cardamom, or ⅛ teaspoon nutmeg, or ¼ teaspoon coriander for each ½ cup portion.

Stir-Fried Carrots

1 PORTION

This method of cooking gives carrots a chewiness you'll love.

2 carrots
2 tablespoons vegetable oil
⅛ teaspoon cumin or marjoram or fennel seed (crushed), or ¼ teaspoon fresh ginger, minced or grated
1 tablespoon soy sauce
1 tablespoon cornstarch

Slice the pieces of carrot into discs ¼ inch thick. Heat 2 tablespoons oil in a wok or heavy skillet. Add the carrot slices and cook in the oil for about 6 minutes, stirring constantly. Season with one of the spices, and remove from the pan.

Make a paste of the soy sauce and cornstarch. Add this mixture to the pan once the carrots have been removed. Stir quickly while scraping the bottom of the pan. Then cook, stirring slowly, for about 1 minute. Return the carrots to the pan and coat with the soy sauce mixture. Serve.

CAULIFLOWER

This sturdy vegetable will keep for more than a week in the crisper.

Because it is so bland, cauliflower is often used to complement more dominant flavors. The texture is quite crisp when raw or marinated, but can become mushy when overcooked—something to avoid. Complementary flavors that come to mind with cauliflower are the sharp contrast of vinegar in a marinade, the pungence of cheddar in a sauce, and the aromatic curries which are so often used in Indian cooking.

East Indian Cauliflower

1 PORTION

Note that this dish calls for only cauliflower and spices—almost no water! The spices are added in stages. The mustard seed and turmeric go into the hot butter to permit the release of flavors, and the ginger, cumin, pepper, and paprika go in with the cauliflower. Try adding fresh or frozen green peas during the last 5 minutes of cooking. Use a pan with a tight lid.

2 tablespoons vegetable oil (or, to be authentic, clarified butter)
1 tablespoon mustard seed
¼ teaspoon turmeric
½ cauliflower head, broken into florets
¼ teaspoon powdered ginger or ½ teaspoon fresh ginger
1 teaspoon cumin
pinch paprika
pinch pepper
¼ teaspoon salt
⅛ cup water

Heat the oil in the pan, then add the mustard seed to the oil. The seeds will begin to explode so watch out for splattering. Once the seeds begin to explode, add the turmeric and stir it thoroughly into the oil. Cook for 15–20 seconds. Add the cauliflower and stir thoroughly to coat it with the spicy oil.

Add the remaining spices and salt and pepper and coat the cauliflower. Add the water and cook over high heat until boiling, then reduce the heat to low, and cover. The cauliflower should be done in 8–10 minutes.

CORN

Fresh corn is at its nutritional best for one or two days. Frozen corn on the cob is frequently available in the supermarket and is a good way to have this treat on hand. Also, frozen corn kernels are handy when packed in plastic bags. You can use what you need while keeping the rest of the bag frozen. Finally, those of you who liked creamed corn will be pleased to learn that it is the most nutritious of the canned corn varieties.

Corn Casserole

This is a very comforting evening meal. Serve it with biscuits and honey.

1 teaspoon whole wheat flour
⅓ cup milk
1 egg, beaten
1 teaspoon butter
½ cup corn kernels
⅛ teaspoon salt
⅛ teaspoon nutmeg
⅛ teaspoon pepper

Preheat the oven to 350° F.

Measure the flour into a saucepan and slowly add the milk, stirring constantly to avoid lumping. Then stir in the beaten egg. Add the remaining ingredients, pour into an ungreased, single-portion casserole dish with a 1½-cup capacity, and bake for 45 minutes. Test for doneness by inserting a knife into the center. The knife should come out clean. Serve hot.

CUCUMBERS

When deciding what to do with a cucumber, consider its most dominant qualities. This will help you to enhance its natural flavor and texture or find a suitable complement. Taking the cucumber as a whole (since you really should not peel it), it is crisp with a cool moistness we associate with melons. Its flavor is extremely subtle with an aftertaste bordering on bitterness contributed by the skin. By running the tines of a fork along the outside of a cucumber in neat lengthwise rows you neutralize some of the bitterness and add a decorative touch as well.

To make a quick cold cucumber soup, finely chop a tomato and a cucumber and add to 1 cup yogurt. Thin with milk to a soup-like consistency. Season with ¼ teaspoon coriander.

Cucumbers in marinade. Because of their neutral flavor and fleshy, moist texture, cucumbers accept marination very well, especially when peeled, seeded, and drained. To marinate, prepare a mixture of 3 tablespoons vinegar, 2 tablespoons vegetable oil, 1 crushed garlic clove, and ¼ teaspoon crushed dill seed. Immerse the cucumber in the marinade and chill for 24 hours. Marinated cucumber can be kept refrigerated for up to two weeks when placed in either the original marinade or a solution of 2 tablespoons vinegar and 1 cup water.

Cucumber and melon. Cucumbers are welcome in any melon salad when peeled for textural consistency.

Tzadziki

This cucumber and yogurt salad is a popular Greek side dish. The garlic and dill bring freshness and creaminess to complement the slight tartness of plain yogurt.

The cucumbers must be seeded, peeled, and drained to minimize any wateriness. Eat the trimmings as a snack, if you like.

Leftover tzadziki will keep for four days in a covered container in the refrigerator.

½ **cucumber, seeded, peeled, and chopped**
1 **8-ounce container plain yogurt**
2 **garlic cloves, crushed**
1 **teaspoon dill weed**
⅛ **teaspoon salt**

The cucumber should drain in a strainer for about 15 minutes. While the cucumber is draining, combine the remaining ingredients. Then stir in the cucumber and serve.

❦COLD RICE SALAD❦

If your rice is gummy and white, use it to make soup. The rice that makes excellent cold salads is long-grain brown rice which has been cooked (but *not* boiled) in water or broth until each grain is separate, plump, and perfect.

Usually a good rice salad is only lightly dressed, if at all. Its appeal lies in the blending of ingredients and textures. To create your own cold rice salad recipe, draw from the following list of ingredients:

chili peppers, canned or fresh
peas, raw or cooked
chopped bell pepper
water chestnuts
dry mustard
minced ginger
raisins
sautéed mushrooms
fish filet
capers
chopped apple

shrimp
chicken
peanuts
pecans
walnuts
currants
chopped celery
chopped onion
chopped green onion
sardines in oil
steamed zucchini discs
grated Parmesan cheese
California black olives
diced brick cheese

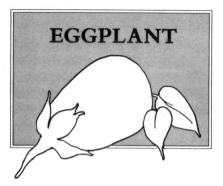

EGGPLANT

The French, English, and East Indians call this vegetable aubergine (oh' bur zheen'). Selecting an eggplant is easy. Look for the prettiest, shiniest one, and you can't go wrong. Size isn't important with regard to quality, so don't hesitate to pick out some small ones.

The eggplant pulp has a sturdy fleshy quality which keeps its shape when cooked. Its subtle flavor provides an outstanding backdrop for a wide range of spices, sauces, and cheeses.

Salting the eggplant is an interesting procedure which draws *from* the eggplant, rather than contributing saltiness *to* it. The principle is that salt is thirsty for moisture; placing salt on the surface draws this moisture from the pulp of the eggplant, and along with it is carried the bitterness that is sometimes present. This prepares the eggplant to absorb the liquid from sauces you add.

Slice the eggplant into ⅜-inch slices, place on a countertop or plate, and liberally cover the eggplant with salt. Use 4–5 tablespoons, depending on the size of the eggplant. After 15 minutes, scrape, turn, and resalt the eggplant, this time on the second side. After 15 minutes, scrape away all the salt, but don't rinse it off— you don't want the eggplant to absorb more water after all the trouble you've taken!

Stuffed Eggplant

You needn't stuff both halves of the eggplant unless you're really hungry or want to have leftovers. There are ample uses for the unstuffed half if you want variety.

½ medium-sized eggplant, sliced lengthwise
¼ cup chopped onion
1 garlic clove, minced
1 tablespoon vegetable oil (olive oil preferred)
1 tomato, chopped
1 carrot, grated
2 tablespoons sesame seed
¼ teaspoon oregano
¼ teaspoon thyme
¼ teaspoon basil
¼ cup grated cheese (Swiss, Jack, or cheddar)
3 tablespoons grated Parmesan cheese

Preheat the oven to 350° F.
Hollow out the eggplant half, leaving ¼ inch of eggplant flesh as a shell. Dice the eggplant pulp.

Sauté the onion, garlic, and eggplant dice in the hot oil. Add the tomato and carrot and cook over low heat with a lid for 6–7 minutes.

Add the sesame seed and spices, then stir in the ¼ cup cheese. Fill the eggplant shell with this mixture. Top with the Parmesan cheese. Place any leftover filling in the base of the baking dish and set the eggplant on top. Bake for 25 minutes. Serve.

Variation

Sauté the diced eggplant with ½ cup sliced mushrooms. Mix with ¼ cup cooked rice and 2 tablespoons chopped raisins. Spice with ½ teaspoon coriander and ⅛ teaspoon turmeric.

Sautéed Eggplant Medley

This recipe is a cousin of rata-touille. It was born on an evening when I was out of zucchini and olives, ingredients essential to rata-touille. The need to use up half an eggplant combined with a yen for the smell of garlic sautéing in olive oil. A sampling of vegetables from the crisper and some crushed marjoram produced a tasty and fast-cooking result much to my liking—and I hope to yours.

Leftovers can be kept for three days in a closed container in the refrigerator.

2 tablespoons olive oil
1 garlic clove, thinly sliced
½ small eggplant, cubed
½ yellow onion, cut in wedges
½ green pepper, cut in strips
2 medium-sized tomatoes, cut in wedges
¼ teaspoon marjoram
pinch pepper

Heat the oil to *hot* and add the garlic. Stir quickly to brown lightly, then add the eggplant cubes and stir to coat. Sauté for 2–3 minutes. Add the onion and green pepper and stir, also over high heat. Finally, add the tomato wedges, marjoram, and pepper and reduce the heat to medium-low. If there is no liquid in the bottom of the pan, add about ¼ cup of water to prevent the vegetables from burning. Simmer covered for 15 minutes and serve.

Duxelles

The essence of mushrooms is brought out by cooking away the water they contain. The result of this recipe is little packets of amazing flavor which can be used when you want to enhance a sauce or gravy or perk up a plain broth.

1 large yellow onion
1 tablespoon butter
2 tablespoons olive oil
1½ cups finely chopped mushrooms
¼ teaspoon nutmeg

Chop the onion very finely. Melt the butter and olive oil in a sauté pan. Add the onion and cook until it is brown. Add the mushrooms and cook until they stop steaming, about 10 minutes. Stir in the nutmeg. Cool. Divide the duxelles into 2-tablespoon portions and wrap them neatly in squares of aluminum foil or plastic wrap to be frozen for future use.

Mushroom Timbale

Very delicate, this pudding is quite simple to make. Serve it piping hot— plain or topped with Béchamel Sauce, p. 182.

12–15 medium-sized mushrooms, chopped
1½ tablespoons butter
pinch nutmeg
pinch salt
pinch pepper
1 egg
¼ cup breadcrumbs
⅓ cup milk

Preheat the oven to 375° F.
Sauté the mushrooms briefly in the melted butter until heated through.

Season with nutmeg, salt, and pepper. Pour the mushrooms into a blender and add the remaining ingredients. Process until smooth, 30 seconds or less, and pour the contents into a greased casserole dish. Bake for 30–40 minutes.

Test for doneness by inserting a sharp knife into the center of the timbale. The dish will be done when the knife comes out clean. Loosen the sides of the timbale and invert onto a plate.

Mushroom Tart

This little pie is both subtle and rich. You can double the recipe, but you probably won't be able to eat it all! Note the simple assembly technique. The tart is akin to both the quiche and the frittata, since an egg custard gives form to the dish.

Use a small pie pan 1½ inches deep, 3 inches wide at the base, and 4½ inches wide at the top, like those that contain individual frozen pies, or any oven container of 1½-cup capacity.

¼ Flaky Pastry recipe, p. 162
12–15 medium-sized mushrooms, sliced
1½ tablespoons butter
⅛ teaspoon marjoram
1 egg
½ cup milk
¼ cup (scant) grated Swiss cheese

Preheat the oven to 350° F.
Line the baking dish with the Flaky Pastry.

Sauté the mushroom slices in butter and season them with the marjoram. Place them in the baking dish. Beat the egg with the milk. Pour the egg mixture over the mushrooms and top with the grated cheese. Gently pat the cheese to submerge it. Bake for 35–40 minutes or until a knife inserted into the center of the tart comes out clean. Serve.

Mushrooms Bombay

This very spicy recipe makes excellent use of mushroom caps. Paprika and cardamom are featured in a rare combination, and the mushrooms are baked before they're sautéed. While the recipe is a three-step process, it really is simple, as are the ingredients. Try this dish with the Potato Frittata (p. 97) and a broiled tomato.

5–7 large mushroom caps
½ teaspoon vegetable oil
3 tablespoons butter, melted
2 tablespoons plain yogurt
pinch cardamom
¼ teaspoon paprika

Preheat the oven to 400° F.
Wipe the mushroom caps clean with a paper towel. Then rub them with the oil. Bake them on a cookie sheet for 20 minutes.

In a mixing bowl, combine 1½ tablespoons of the melted butter with the yogurt. Coat the baked mushrooms with the sauce.

In a small pan combine the remaining 1½ tablespoons melted butter with the spices. Heat through. Add the mushrooms and stir. Cook over a low heat for 10 minutes. Serve immediately.

Mushroom and Spinach Stuffed Tomatoes

This dish has a lovely presentation. To make it for guests, you may double everything.

1 tablespoon minced onion
4 medium-sized mushrooms, chopped, with 2 caps reserved
1 garlic clove, crushed
1 tablespoon butter, melted
¼ pound fresh spinach, cooked and chopped, or ½ 10-ounce package frozen chopped spinach, thawed and drained
1 egg, slightly beaten
2 tablespoons grated Parmesan cheese
⅛ teaspoon thyme
pinch pepper
tomato pulp
2 tomatoes, hollowed out

Preheat the oven to 325° F.
Sauté the onion, mushrooms, and garlic in butter. Add the remaining ingredients, except the 2 hollowed-out tomatoes, and mix well. Stuff the tomatoes with the mixture. Oil the 2 mushroom caps and place them on top of the stuffed tomato. Bake in a greased baking dish for 15–20 minutes. Serve.

Andrea's Marinated Mushrooms

When mushrooms are young (less ripe) their caps hug the stem, like a closed umbrella. As they develop, the "umbrella," or cap, opens. Unopened mushrooms are preferred in this recipe because opened mushrooms are more fragile. The gills are exposed on the underside of the cap, and they break off very easily. Also, the cap itself breaks off in pieces, which is less attractive than the effect of unopened mushrooms.

½ **pound fresh mushrooms, unopened**
½ **cup vegetable oil**
¼ **cup red wine vinegar**
1 **tablespoon lemon juice**
½ **teaspoon tarragon**
1 **garlic clove, minced**
½ **teaspoon salt**
¼ **teaspoon granulated sugar**

Combine all the ingredients and marinate the mushrooms overnight in the refrigerator.

Baked Onion

While it's true that onions are tamed during cooking, they are still flavorful and have a good texture when baked. Select a small casserole dish for baking. If it doesn't have a lid, you will need to fashion one from foil. Grease the casserole dish.

1 **medium-sized yellow onion, cut in half across the middle**
2 **tablespoons water**
¾ **cup Basic White Sauce, p. 177**

Preheat the oven to 375° F.
Place the onion halves, cut-side up, in the greased casserole dish. Add the water and cover the dish. Bake for 30 minutes. Then top with the white sauce and bake uncovered for 10 more minutes. The onion halves should be tender. Serve.

Variation

Slice a whole yellow onion into thirds. Butter all the cut surfaces. Lightly sprinkle each buttered surface with soy sauce. Reassemble the onion and wrap it in a square of aluminum foil, crimping the edges together to prevent the escape of steam. Place on a grill over hot coals and test for doneness after 35 minutes. Continue baking until done to your taste. The onion can also be baked in a 350° F. oven for 45 minutes.

PEAS

Fresh peas are a fine treat, even more so because when refrigerated in the pod, they keep for over a month. Rarely are fresh peas available in the market, however. The alternative is to keep frozen peas on hand and pour out as many as needed, leaving the rest frozen.

Fresh or frozen green peas don't need much cooking. If they are heated to the steaming point, then shocked in cold water, the brightness will be preserved along with the texture.

East Indian Peas

1 PORTION

Turmeric and coriander are probably among the most popular spices in India. In this surprising recipe, the peas are bathed in these spices and cooked in almost no water. The method is very effective, and the peas prove equal to the occasion.

Clarify the butter to keep it from burning as the peas cook. Do this by melting 2½ tablespoons butter and skimming off all the bubbly residue. The 2 tablespoons of clear liquid fat is what you want.

Select a saucepan with a lid for stovetop cooking.

2 tablespoons clarified butter
¼ teaspoon turmeric
1-1½ cups peas, fresh or frozen
½ teaspoon coriander
pinch salt
2 teaspoons water

Heat the clarified butter and add the turmeric to it, stirring to blend. Add the peas and stir to coat, then gently stir for an additional 2 minutes. Add the coriander and salt, and stir for 1 minute more. Add 2 teaspoons water to the pan all at once and cover. This will raise a quick head of steam, and you'll want to put the lid on the pan right away. Steam for 2–3 minutes. Serve hot.

Variation

Add 1 8-ounce container of plain yogurt once the peas have completed cooking, and serve as a main dish.

Peas with Mint

Here is a trick to use when cooking with herbs. Warm the herbs in milk to bring out the flavor. The oil from the herb blends with the fat in the milk, and the heat brings the flavor to life. Here, dried mint leaves are crushed and sprinkled into the milk in which the peas are cooked.

¾–1 cup fresh or frozen peas
½ teaspoon dried mint leaves
½ cup milk

Add the peas and mint to the simmering milk and cook covered for 3 minutes or less, until the peas are steaming. Serve immediately.

Potato Frittata

This could become a standard in your repertoire since it can be eaten at any meal. Potatoes and eggs are the only required ingredients. The rest is only suggested, and can be varied according to your own taste. The frittata can be cooked on stovetop over low heat, or baked in the oven. Leftover frittata is good cold, so don't overlook it as a bag lunch or picnic entrée.

¾–1 cup diced new potato
1 tablespoon butter
1–2 tablespoons diced green pepper
1 tablespoon diced onion
1–2 mushrooms, sliced
½ teaspoon pepper
¼ teaspoon salt
¼ teaspoon marjoram
¼ teaspoon basil
2 teaspoons grated Parmesan cheese
2 tablespoons milk
2 eggs, slightly beaten

In a saucepan, bring ½ inch of water to a boil, add the potato dice, and cook for 7 minutes. Drain. In a frying pan, melt the butter and sauté the green pepper, onion, and mushrooms until tender. Add the pepper, salt, marjoram, and basil. Add the drained potatoes to the frittata pan and sprinkle with Parmesan cheese.

Combine the milk with the eggs. Stir briskly with a fork until mixed. To prevent the egg mixture from sticking, you may want to add a little more butter to coat the bottom of the pan. Pour the egg mixture over the vegetables and cook uncovered over medium-low heat until set. You may want to cover the pan during the last 2 minutes to set the very top center. Invert the frittata onto a plate and serve.

German Potato Pancakes

This very substantial pancake takes a while to cook as pancakes go, but it's certainly worth the trouble. You'll make a simple mixture of egg and flour, then grate onion and potato directly into it. You may want to measure the first time you try this recipe.

Leftover pancakes can be reheated. Try them with applesauce.

1 egg, slightly beaten
2 tablespoons whole wheat flour
pinch salt
2 tablespoons grated onion
1 russet potato, scrubbed, not peeled
3 tablespoons butter, melted

Beat the egg and the flour together in a small bowl. Salt lightly. Grate the onion into this mixture by using the fine section of your grater. Then grate the potato directly into the batter, using the larger grating size. Mix thoroughly.

Melt the butter in a skillet. This mixture doesn't readily assume a pancake shape, so just glop the mounds onto the cooking surface and pat them into shape. Let the pancakes cook over medium heat for about 10 minutes on each side, turning them when golden brown.

Variation

Pancakes may be baked at 425° F. for 35–40 minutes, or until golden and crisp.

❧ LEFTOVER COOKED POTATO ❧

Pommes de Terre Hareng. Slice chilled potato onto a salad plate. Lightly drizzle with olive oil and sprinkle with crushed basil, salt, and pepper. Serve with canned herring or sardines.

Potato soup. Sauté ¼ cup combined celery and onion in a soup pot. Add diced potato and enough milk to make the mixture soupy, and heat through. Season with salt and pepper. If desired, mash the mixture to thicken it. Caraway is an interesting and tasty seasoning for potato soup.

Hash-browned potatoes. Melt 1 tablespoon butter in a skillet. Add thinly sliced or grated potato and fry until desired texture—from just heated through to golden brown. Pepper to taste.

Potato salad. Combine potato dice with enough mayonnaise to moisten. Add chopped salad vegetables on hand: celery, onion, olives, grated carrot. Season with celery seed, salt, mustard, pepper, and herbs (dill seed, oregano, or tarragon).

Cold plate. Arrange potato slices with artichoke hearts, hard-cooked eggs, beet slices, and tomato wedges. Dress with a vinaigrette of 3 tablespoons white vinegar, ⅛ teaspoon prepared mustard, minced garlic, 1 teaspoon fresh parsley, and ¼ cup vegetable oil. Serve.

Scalloped Potato

Choose a small russet potato and a small yellow onion, and you can eat this dish in one sitting. If you make a larger amount, leftovers can be turned into a delectable potato soup enhanced by corn kernels and fresh pepper.

Select a baking dish to hold about 2 cups, and grease it.

1 small potato
1 small onion
1 tablespoon unbleached, all-purpose flour
⅛ teaspoon oregano
pinch salt
⅛ teaspoon pepper
½ cup milk
2 teaspoons butter

Preheat the oven to 350° F.

Thinly slice both the potato and the onion. Make a mixture of the flour, oregano, salt, and pepper.

After layering about 2 onion and 2 potato slices in the baking dish, coat with a thin layer of flour and add another potato-onion layer. Repeat this process until all the ingredients have been added. Finish with an onion slice on top.

Add the milk, dot with 2 teaspoons butter, and bake uncovered for 30 minutes. Remove from the oven and serve hot.

Stuffed Baked Potato

This portable treat is just right for winter outings, ballgames, or a bagged lunch. Should you want to save half for future eating, you can either freeze it, wrapped securely in foil or plastic wrap, or store it in the refrigerator for use within the next two or three days. The potato is delicious when reheated at 325° F. for 20 minutes and topped with grated Parmesan cheese.

1 baked potato, cooled
1 tablespoon butter
2 tablespoons milk, or as needed
⅛ teaspoon pepper
2 tablespoons grated cheddar cheese or cream cheese or ricotta cheese
2 tablespoons chopped ham or crumbled bacon, or sautéed sausage, optional

Cut the potato in half lengthwise and gently remove the cooked potato to a mixing bowl, taking care to preserve the shape of the skin. Add the butter, milk, and pepper and mix until light and smooth. Stir in the cheese and chopped meat. Divide the mixture in half and return it to the hollow potato halves. Serve right away or wrap to take out or save.

Gnocchi Verdi

This recipe features a popular Italian combination: spinach and ricotta cheese. The dough is held together with flour and egg, and the little dumplings are cooked in gently boiling water. They are then topped with melted butter and grated Parmesan cheese and may be broiled for a few minutes before serving.

Ricotta is usually sold in 1-pound containers yielding about 1¾ cups of cheese. Once opened, the cheese should be used within two or three days, so you'll need to plan a bit. Try using the leftover ricotta in a lasagna or as stuffing for manicotti; you can freeze individual portions for later use. Reserve some of the ricotta for use in scrambled eggs and frittatas.

Leftover gnocchi can be frozen and later reheated in a 350° F. oven for 15–20 minutes or until hot. Top with grated Parmesan cheese to keep them from drying out while baking. If you don't freeze leftover gnocchi, keep them refrigerated and use them within four days.

½ cup ricotta cheese
1 egg, slightly beaten
pinch salt
2 tablespoons grated Parmesan cheese
½ pound fresh spinach, cooked and chopped, or 1 10-ounce package frozen chopped spinach, thawed and drained
3 tablespoons unbleached, all-purpose flour
1 tablespoon butter, melted

Choose a large, deep frying pan or saucepan, fill three-quarters full with water, and bring to a boil. Reduce to a simmer.

In a mixing bowl combine the ricotta, egg, salt, and Parmesan cheese. Add the drained spinach and mix. With a tablespoon, form individual balls of dough. Roll each ball in the flour until coated, then gently drop it into the simmering water. Cook for 5 minutes or until the gnocchi rise to the top of the water. Remove from the water with a slotted spoon, top with the melted butter and more Parmesan cheese, and serve.

Variation

You can broil the gnocchi once they have finished poaching if you wish. Preheat the broiler for 5 minutes. Place the cooked gnocchi on an ovenproof plate, top with melted butter, and sprinkle with Parmesan cheese. Broil for 3–5 minutes, or until golden brown.

SUMMER SQUASH

These fast-growing varieties of squash are light and tasty when properly cooked. From June through August, crookneck, cymling, and zucchini squashes are abundant and cheap. If you are not yet a squash aficionado, perhaps the right recipe hasn't come your way. Don't pass up the chance to enjoy these great vegetables. The trick is not to let them overcook.

All varieties of summer squash are best when used within three to five days of purchase.

Stuffed Zucchini

The stuffing is cooked separately, then placed in the raw zucchini halves for baking. The result is an al dente delight. The stuffing is fresh and sweet.

Select a medium-sized zucchini tending to wide. Cut it in half lengthwise and hollow out the inside pulp by cutting a valley down the center with a sharp knife.

Leftovers may be frozen and reheated in a 350° F. oven for 20–25 minutes or until hot. If not frozen, refrigerate and eat within four days.

1 tablespoon chopped onion
1 garlic clove, chopped fine
chopped zucchini pulp
1 tablespoon olive oil
2 tablespoons grated carrot
1 tomato, diced
1 tablespoon chopped walnuts or pecans
⅛ teaspoon basil
1 medium-sized zucchini, hollowed out
1 tablespoon breadcrumbs or grated Parmesan cheese

Preheat the oven to 350° F.

Sauté the onion, garlic, and zucchini pulp in the olive oil until the onion is translucent. Don't let the garlic burn. Add the carrot, tomato, nuts, and basil, and stir to mix. Simmer until the tomato is heated through.

Divide the mixture in half and spoon into the hollow zucchini halves. Top with the breadcrumbs or grated Parmesan cheese. Bake in a covered dish for 25–30 minutes or until the zucchini is tender but not soggy. Serve.

Cymling Frittata with Fennel

This is the most delicate presentation of a frittata ever. The texture of the squash is perfect, and the fresh fennel gives off a subtle, full-bodied bouquet which is a perfect complement to the dish.

You may substitute zucchini or crookneck squash for the cymling.

1 cymling squash, cut into discs
6 thin slices Swiss cheese
6–8 mushrooms, sliced and sautéed
2 teaspoons fresh fennel or ⅛ teaspoon crushed fennel seed
2 teaspoons chopped parsley
2 eggs, slightly beaten
1 cup milk
pinch salt
pinch pepper

Preheat the oven to 350° F.

Butter a baking dish of about 2-cup capacity, and layer the squash, cheese slices, and sautéed mushrooms, sprinkling the layers evenly with fennel and chopped parsley.

Combine the eggs, milk, salt, and pepper and pour over the squash. Bake for 35 minutes, or until a knife inserted into the center comes out clean. Serve hot.

Crookneck Squash Gratin

This is a delicious light-textured dish flavored with a good cheddar cheese. Plan ahead by cooking a whole crookneck squash, covered, in boiling water for 15 minutes. Allow to cool.

1 egg, separated
2 tablespoons sour cream
1½ tablespoons unbleached, all-purpose flour
1 crookneck squash, cooked, sliced thin
⅓ cup grated cheddar cheese

Preheat the oven to 350° F.

Beat the egg yolk. Add the sour cream, then the flour, and mix thoroughly. Beat the egg white to stiff, but not dry, peaks and fold into the yolk mixture.

In a buttered individual casserole dish with a 1½-cup capacity, layer half the squash, egg mixture, and cheese. Then repeat, ending with the last half of the cheese.

Bake for 20–25 minutes and serve.

CHICKEN
&
RED MEAT

In this chapter you will find recipes for the cuts of chicken and so-called red meat commonly sold in grocery stores and butcher shops. My own preference, which is consistent with national health goals, is to eat red meat only occasionally, and to rely on chicken, fish, and non-meat sources for protein. You will find this bias reflected throughout the book and in this chapter, particularly, which is weighted in favor of chicken recipes. The chicken recipes come first and are followed by recipes for a variety of red meats.

CHICKEN

You can do anything you want with chicken! It is by far the most versatile member of the meat/poultry group. It can be cut into chunks like stew meat, pounded flat à la veal scaloppine, braised, broiled, stuffed, or roasted on or off the bone. It can even be ground into patties. Feature chicken in an elegant meal or make it the basic fare in an all-American picnic.

There need never be any waste with chicken, because its size makes it manageable. For people cooking for one, a chicken is as big as a week. Even if you don't eat it every day, you can plan its use realistically, freezing some, refrigerating some, and cooking the rest.

You may want to buy a whole chicken just to have the challenge of using it well and economically. Each piece of chicken is best used in a certain way: wings are delicious stir-fried, thighs are succulent when sautéed or baked in a sauce, backs are good stewed. The breast can be boned and skinned, then frozen for a time when you want to make a tasty stuffed boneless breast, scaloppine style.

Chicken Sauté

This is the simplest way to cook chicken pieces. There is no dredging in flour, no special sauce. This is the sauté technique at its plainest. When you select your chicken pieces, be aware that light meat such as breast meat cooks faster than dark meat.

You're going to add the chicken to hot oil, which will seal in the juices. Guard against splatters by towel-drying the rinsed chicken first.

1 tablespoon vegetable oil
2–3 chicken pieces, rinsed and patted dry

Over medium heat, heat the oil. Place the chicken skin-side down in the skillet for 10 minutes. Turn and cook for 20 more minutes. If you are cooking a thigh and a breast, place the thigh in the pan first and brown it on one side for about 8 minutes before adding the breast. Turn the thigh, add the breast skin-side down, and continue to sauté over medium heat for 8 minutes. Then turn the breast and cook for 15 more minutes.

To check for doneness, pierce the chicken with a fork; the chicken is done when the juices flow clear. (Some people prefer the juice to be **slightly pink**.)

❧TO BONE A CHICKEN BREAST❧

If you have a whole breast, begin at the midsection and cut gently away from the bone, from the center down, on each side next to the midbone. Once the meat is free from the bone, you may want to skin it. Pull the skin off where unattached or loosely attached. In those places where it is firmly attached, insert a sharp knife between the skin and the flesh and work the skin free. The chicken breast, now in two pieces, is ready to cook, refrigerate for up to three days, or freeze. (Recipes which call for a chicken breast refer to one of these pieces.)

Chicken Sauté Sec

This is one way of embellishing the basic Chicken Sauté. Notice that flavorings are added in a variety of ways: first to the oil with garlic, then to the chicken skin via the flavored oil, finally to the pan juices once the chicken is cooked. Just imagine the many variations available to you. You could sprinkle crushed herbs on the chicken as it cooks. A sauce could be made by squeezing a lemon into the pan juices; or, cream or half-and-half could be added and reduced to a thick sauce. That sauce could be further seasoned with curry powder. Once you have tried this recipe once or twice, experiment by using your own favorites.

This recipe is called Chicken Sauté Sec because it uses dry white wine— "sec" is the French word for dry. It is not necessary to use wine, however; lemon juice works nicely, as does broth. Should you be cooking both breasts and thighs, note the special instructions for this in Chicken Sauté, p. 106.

1 tablespoon vegetable oil
1 garlic clove, peeled and sliced
2–3 chicken pieces, rinsed and patted dry
1 tablespoon butter
pinch sage
¼ cup dry white wine or broth, or 2 tablespoons lemon juice

Over medium heat, heat the oil in a frying pan and add the garlic to it, stirring briefly. (If the oil is so hot that the garlic browns immediately, reduce the heat and remove the garlic—it must not burn.) Add the chicken to the pan, still over medium heat, and cook for 8 minutes on each side. Remove the chicken to a plate. Discard the garlic and all but 1 tablespoon of the pan oil.

Add the butter, melt it, add the sage, and stir briefly. Then add the white wine and stir again until the wine bubbles. If you add broth or lemon juice, do the same. Return the chicken to the pan, coat it with the sauce, and simmer covered for about 15 minutes. To check for doneness, pierce the chicken with a fork; the chicken is done when the juices flow clear.

Chicken Casserole

This recipe produces a lovely, golden brown chicken that is moist and juicy after about 30 minutes of cooking. Should you be cooking both breasts and thighs, note the special instructions for this in Chicken Sauté p. 106. Use the dredging step as an additional seal for the chicken juices and as a source of flavoring. It isn't essential, however, and you will see that there are plenty of other ways to flavor your chicken. If you want to have gravy, see Chicken Gravy, p. 185.

To fry the chicken, select a heavy skillet with a lid to hold both chicken and vegetables.

3 tablespoons whole wheat flour
⅛ teaspoon salt
⅛ teaspoon pepper
¼ teaspoon basil
¼ teaspoon thyme
2–3 chicken pieces, rinsed and patted dry
2 tablespoons vegetable oil
1½ cups chopped raw vegetables

Combine the flour, salt, pepper, and herbs and dredge the chicken in the mixture.

Heat the oil in a skillet until it is hot but not smoking. Add the chicken pieces, skin-side down, and fry until golden brown (5–7 minutes). Turn and fry an additional 7 minutes over medium heat. Then reduce the heat and add the vegetables.

Cover and cook for about 20 minutes. If you're using a combination of vegetables, consider their relative cooking times. Root vegetables such as carrots and turnips would have to be sliced very thin to cook in 20 minutes alongside broccoli, zucchini, or other lighter vegetables.

Variations

- Chicken and zucchini (1-inch pieces), seasoned with basil, tarragon, thyme, or fennel seed, and topped with soy sauce.
- Chicken and tomato wedges, seasoned with dill weed (or tarragon, garlic, and pepper), and topped with Parmesan cheese, yogurt, or sour cream.
- Chicken and mushroom caps (whole or sliced), seasoned with paprika and oregano. White wine or sour cream added to the pan juices will make a sauce.
- Chicken and red or green cabbage with caraway seed and lemon juice.
- Chicken with green peas and onion wedges, seasoned with mint and marjoram, and topped with lemon juice and melted butter, or Basic White Sauce (p. 177).
- Chicken and paper-thin lemon slices, seasoned with tarragon. Dry vermouth or white wine could be added just after the chicken is browned.
- Chicken and potato cubes, seasoned with parsley, rosemary, and pepper.

This recipe has its origins in East Indian cuisine, where yogurt is frequently a companion to chicken. Many recipes call for the marination of chicken in yogurt for up to 18 hours. Whether or not the yogurt is used as a marinade, the chicken is skinned, pierced (and boned, if possible) to permit the best penetration of flavors into the chicken and to eliminate an excess of rendered chicken fat in the food.

In braising, chicken is first sautéed, then cooked for 35–40 minutes while semi-immersed in liquid. Here, the liquid is yogurt. One great advantage to braising is the rich broth or sauce which is produced.

2 tablespoons vegetable oil
1 tablespoon butter
½ onion, finely chopped
2 garlic cloves, minced
1 teaspoon grated fresh ginger,
    or ½ teaspoon ground ginger
⅛ teaspoon cardamom
⅛ teaspoon ground cloves
1 bay leaf
1 teaspoon coriander
pinch cayenne
½ cup plain yogurt
1–2 chicken breasts, skinned and
    boned
¼ cup heavy cream

Combine the oil and butter in a skillet with a lid. Add the onion, garlic, and ginger and stir until the onion begins to brown. Add the spices, stir for about 15 seconds, then add the yogurt 2 tablespoons at a time. Make sure the excess moisture has evaporated before each addition. When all the yogurt is added, place the boned chicken in the yogurt mixture to coat, and cook until the chicken is no longer pink.

Reduce the heat and place a lid on the pan. Cook for 25 minutes, stirring occasionally. When the time is up, add the cream, stir, let stand for 10 minutes, and serve.

Oriental Chicken

Marinating is an almost effortless way to produce a very flavorful meal. These marinated chicken thighs will broil in about 25 minutes, so choose a vegetable that cooks in less time than that. Steam some asparagus or snowpeas in spring and summer, or make a hearty crudité vinaigrette. While mashed potatoes aren't very oriental, they round out a nice hot meal.

3 tablespoons Worcestershire sauce
juice of 1 lemon
¼ teaspoon fennel seed, crushed
¼ teaspoon ground ginger, or ½ teaspoon minced fresh ginger
2 chicken thighs

Combine all the ingredients, except the chicken, to make a marinade.

Put the chicken in a broiler pan or a small dish and cover with the marinade. If you are home during the day, turn the chicken from time to time as it marinates. Marinate for at least 3 hours.

Preheat the broiler.

Place the marinated chicken on a piece of foil about 6 inches under the hot broiler. Rotate and baste it four times in the 25 minutes it will take to cook. Use tongs to rotate the chicken. If you pierce the chicken by turning it with a fork, the juices will run out, causing the chicken to become dry. Baste with juices and with oil if necessary.

To test for doneness, pierce the chicken with a fork; the chicken is done when the juices run clear. Don't pierce until toward the end of the 25 minutes.

Most general-purpose cookbooks have a "Hungarian" or a "paprika" recipe, usually interchangeable, which demonstrates the use of paprika as a flavorful spice as opposed to a garnish. This is a pretty vast oversimplification of the complex Hungarian cuisine, which incorporates several kinds of paprika of varying strengths, all a vivid red and visually indistinguishable.

What follows is my own oversimplification of Hungarian cooking, delicious nevertheless, which is certain to heighten your appreciation of paprika. You needn't stick to chicken, either. Try veal, or use sliced mushrooms instead of meat.

½ **onion, chopped fine**
2 **tablespoons vegetable oil or butter**
2 **chicken pieces**
2 **teaspoons paprika**
½ **teaspoon celery salt**
¼ **teaspoon pepper**
1 **tomato, chopped fine**
½ **cup water**
1 **tablespoon unbleached, all-purpose flour**
¼ **cup sour cream**

Sauté the onion in the hot oil or butter. Brown the chicken and remove it from the pan. Add the spices, stirring briefly in the pan juices.

Then add the tomato and ¼ cup of the water and simmer for 5 minutes. Return the chicken to the pan and simmer for 30 minutes.

Remove the chicken to a platter. Add the flour to the pan juices and increase the heat to medium. Cook to thicken, about 2 minutes, and gradually whisk in the remaining ¼ cup water. The sauce should be the consistency of thick gravy. Simmer for about 1 minute, then whisk in the sour cream and heat through without boiling. Pour the sauce over the chicken and serve.

Nancy's Authentic Chicken Curry

As this dish simmers, your home will become filled with rich scents from the heart of India. Instead of using curry powder, you will add spices to the sautéed chicken one at a time as it is done by the East Indians. The use of chicken thighs is preferable in this recipe since the dark meat, with its higher fat content, accepts the flavoring of the spices more readily than white meat does. Dark meat can also cook longer without overcooking. The chicken is skinned to further enhance the absorption of the aromatics.

2 chicken thighs, skinned (save the skin)
¼ teaspoon turmeric
⅛ teaspoon cumin
¼ teaspoon paprika
⅛ teaspoon ground ginger, or ¼ teaspoon grated fresh ginger
pinch cayenne
½ teaspoon coriander
1 cup water or chicken broth
pinch salt

Select a medium-sized skillet with a lid. Heat the pan to medium-hot and place the chicken skins in the pan. The fat from the skin will begin to melt, or render, into the pan. When about 1 tablespoon of chicken fat has collected on the bottom of the pan, remove the skin and discard it.

Add the chicken thighs and sauté all surfaces quickly. When the chicken is no longer pink, add the turmeric and cumin and continue to sauté until golden brown. Add the paprika, ginger, cayenne, and coriander. Stir for 1 minute.

Slowly add the 1 cup of liquid. If water is used, add salt to taste. Cover and simmer over low heat for 45 minutes. Then serve.

Stir-Fry Chicken Gizzards & Hearts

This is a real down-home meal. It can be made in a wok, Dutch oven, or heavy skillet with a lid. It will be somewhat chewy, as such is the nature of this meat.

1 tablespoon vegetable oil
¾ cup chicken gizzards and hearts, whole or cut in half
1 onion, quartered
1 garlic clove, minced
½ cup broccoli florets or a combination of cauliflower, broccoli, and carrots, sliced thin
1½ tablespoons soy sauce

Heat the oil over medium-high heat and add the gizzards and hearts. Stir briskly for 3–5 minutes until evenly browned. Add the onion, garlic, and broccoli and stir again until the vegetables are coated with oil. Add the soy sauce, stir, cover, and reduce the heat. Cook for 15–20 minutes or until the broccoli is done. Serve.

Baked Chicken in Leftover Sauce

This is an easy way to use up leftover soups and sauces. This method is a form of stewing.

When baking chicken in this way, you may as well bake the rest of your dinner. Quarter a potato lengthwise, oil it, and put it on a cookie sheet. Put it in the oven when you put in the chicken. After 15 minutes, add a zucchini sliced into ¾-inch pieces. In 10 more minutes, pop in a tomato with the top removed and some mushroom caps. Everything will be done at once. ⚘

Chicken à la Senegal

2 cups puréed Mulligatawney (p. 27)

2 chicken breasts

Chicken Marinara

3 tomatoes, halved

1½ cups tomato sauce (spaghetti sauce, for example)

2 chicken pieces

Black Forest Chicken

1 bockwurst, cut into ½-inch pieces

1½ cups Lentil Soup (p. 23)

2–3 chicken pieces

Preheat the oven to 350° F.

Place the chicken (and vegetables or other meats) in a baking dish, season it as you like, then smother it in sauce. Bake it for 45 minutes. Serve.

Chicken Scaloppine Diablo

It's fun to see how easy it is to make something you'd pay for dearly in a restaurant. The chicken can be kept warm in a 200° F. oven while you make the sauce. ⚘

1–2 chicken breasts, skinned and boned

¼ cup whole wheat flour

pinch rosemary

pinch thyme

pinch salt

pinch pepper

2 tablespoons butter

½ cup Sauce Diablo (p. 183)

Place the boned chicken breasts, one at a time, between two pieces of plastic wrap. With a rolling pin or mallet, pound the meat gently and evenly into a patty ¼ inch thick.

Make a mixture of the flour, spices, salt, and pepper. Dredge each piece of chicken in the flour mixture.

Melt the butter in a skillet. Sauté the dredged chicken, 2½ minutes to a side. Pour the sauce over the warm chicken and serve.

Chicken Liver with Sage

This popular Italian recipe is adapted from one in Marcella Hazan's Classic Italian Cookbook. I think it is one of the best uses of chicken livers I have seen. Fresh green beans sprinkled with lemon juice make an excellent companion.

While chicken livers are almost ready to cook when purchased, they do need a little trimming, rinsing, patting, and general shaping up before they hit the pan. Run the livers under cold water, drain them, and pat them dry with towelling. Discard any very "loose" livers that will disintegrate easily. Trim away the fat globules. (Scissors are good for this.) Then the liver is ready to be cooked.

2 tablespoons butter
1 tablespoon finely chopped onion
4–5 chicken livers (⅓–½ cup)
2 teaspoons sage
3 tablespoons white wine or broth
pinch salt
pinch pepper

Preheat the oven to 200° F.

Warm a platter in the oven. Melt the butter in a skillet and sauté the onion until it begins to brown. Add the chicken livers and sage and sauté over high heat until the livers are medium rare, or until the pink juices disappear.

Place the cooked livers on the warm platter in the oven. Add the wine or broth to the pan juices over medium heat and scrape the particles from the bottom of the pan. Once the sauce has reduced to form a slight glaze, return the livers to the pan and coat with the sauce. Stir gently and briefly over high heat, then return to the platter for serving. Salt and pepper to taste.

Chicken Breast Stuffed with Wild Rice and Nuts

This recipe takes a bit of time to prepare. You know it's special because of the wild rice: it's expensive. Of course, you may substitute long-grain brown rice or a packaged combination of the two. For the trouble you are taking, make two breasts. You may or may not have leftovers.

Allow 40 minutes for the rice to cook. As it cooks, prepare the chicken breast, then mix the stuffing when the rice is done. The chicken breast will be wrapped around the stuffing, secured with a toothpick or two, sautéed, and then baked.

½ cup chicken broth or water
¼ cup wild rice or long-grain brown rice
2 tablespoons chopped walnuts, almonds, or pecans
2 mushrooms, minced
1 teaspoon currants or chopped raisins
¼ teaspoon coriander
⅛ teaspoon cinnamon
⅛ teaspoon cumin
pinch salt
pinch pepper
2 chicken breasts, skinned and boned, then pounded thin
2 tablespoons butter
1 teaspoon vegetable oil

Bring the broth to a boil, add the rice, and reduce the heat to low. Put a lid on the pan and cook for 40 minutes. Add the remaining ingredients (except the chicken, butter, and vegetable oil). Cook for 10 more minutes.

Preheat the oven to 350° F.

Spoon 2 tablespoons of the rice into the center of each piece of chicken. Fold the chicken over and secure each end with a toothpick. Melt the butter in the skillet and sauté the chicken until it is golden all over.

Oil a small casserole dish with 1 teaspoon vegetable oil. Spoon the remaining rice into the bottom of the casserole dish. Place the stuffed chicken on top. Bake covered for 20 minutes. Serve.

Stuffed Whole Cornish Hen

Once the stuffing is made, this meal cooks itself, except for occasional basting. The stuffing requires only a couple of pieces of bread, and the recipe can vary greatly. Plan to bake your vegetable alongside the chicken.

1 recipe Basic Stuffing, p. 63
1 Cornish game hen, thawed

Preheat the oven to 350° F.

Remove any organs from the large, lower cavity of the hen. Gently pack the stuffing into the large cavity and the small cavity above the breast. Tie the feet together with a string to keep the breast from cooking too fast.

Place the hen *breast-down* in a small roasting pan or a casserole dish. Any leftover stuffing should be placed in a separate dish for baking. Put the bird in the oven. Baste after 15 minutes and every 10 minutes thereafter. Bake extra stuffing at your leisure, allowing 15 minutes for each ½ cup. Test the bird for doneness after 45 minutes. When the meat is pierced, its juices should run clear.

The stuffing should be removed from the bird *immediately* once baked to prevent growth of harmful bacteria. Any leftover stuffing should be refrigerated and eaten within three days.

Chicken Wings Anna

Something miraculous happens to chicken wings when they're cooked this way. They are transformed from meatless wonders into succulent, plump delicacies. There will be some sauce left in the pan, and it makes a delicious gravy for rice.

Oyster sauce is a sublime concoction available in most Oriental and gourmet specialty shops and even some supermarkets. If unavailable to you, use 2 teaspoons A-1 or Worcestershire sauce.

6 chicken wings
2 tablespoons sesame oil or other vegetable oil
¼ cup sherry
¼ cup water
2 tablespoons soy sauce
2 tablespoons oyster sauce

Rinse and pat dry the chicken wings; then cut them at the second joint, leaving one shorter, fatter piece and one longer, thinner piece. Brown the wings in the oil. Add the sherry, water, and soy sauce and bring to a boil. Cook for 20 minutes over medium heat, allowing the liquid to reduce. Add the oyster sauce, coat, cover to heat through, and serve.

Peppered Shepherd's Pie

Your leftover chicken is bathed in a lemon sauce and mixed with generous wedges of green pepper, then tucked between two soft layers of peppery mashed potatoes laced with rich cream cheese. Wow! Count on 15 minutes to assemble and 15 minutes to bake. The recipe is easily doubled.

½ potato, diced
2 tablespoons milk
2 tablespoons butter
pinch salt
⅛ teaspoon pepper
2 tablespoons cream cheese
2 teaspoons unbleached, all-purpose flour
juice of ½ lemon
3 tablespoons white wine or broth
½ green pepper, cut into large dice
½ cup cooked and diced chicken

Preheat the oven to 350° F.

Place the potato in ½ inch of boiling water, cover, and cook over reduced heat for 8 minutes. Drain, then mash the potato with milk and 1 tablespoon of the butter, the salt and pepper, and the cream cheese. Set aside.

Melt the remaining 1 tablespoon of butter and add the flour to it, making a paste. Squeeze the lemon juice into the pan and whisk. Add the white wine or broth and stir constantly over high heat until the sauce is slightly reduced, about 30 seconds or so. Add the green pepper and stir to coat. Add the chicken and stir again. Turn off the heat.

Spread ⅓ of the mashed potatoes over the bottom of an individual casserole dish. Place the chicken mixture over that and top with the remaining potatoes. Bake for 15 minutes. Serve.

Chicken Fettuccine

Cooked chicken is dressed up in a cream sauce rich with egg yolk, then tossed with hot fettuccine.

Leftovers may be refrigerated and eaten within three days. You may also freeze leftovers and reheat them by baking them covered at 350° F. for 30 minutes or until hot.

4–5 medium-sized mushrooms, sliced thick
3 tablespoons chopped green pepper
2 tablespoons butter, melted
1 tablespoon unbleached, all-purpose flour
1 cup chicken broth
1½ tablespoons sour cream or heavy cream
1 egg yolk
⅛ teaspoon salt
⅛ teaspoon pepper
¾ cup diced, cooked chicken
1 cup cooked fettuccine or other noodle
2 teaspoons butter
2 teaspoons grated Parmesan cheese

Sauté the mushrooms and green pepper in the 2 tablespoons melted butter. Then remove the vegetables from the pan, leaving 1 tablespoon butter. Add the flour to make a paste, then gradually add the chicken broth, whisking constantly.

Combine the cream with the egg yolk. Beat until smooth, then whisk into the broth. Add the salt, pepper, mushrooms, green pepper, and chicken, and simmer gently until heated through. Toss the cooked noodles with the butter and Parmesan cheese. Pour the chicken and sauce over the noodles and serve.

Herbed Chicken Breast

This is the basis for many fine chicken recipes. The breast is skinned, boned, and cut into cubes about 1 inch square. The cubes are dredged in an herbed flour, then sautéed in butter until golden, cooking in just minutes. The chicken stays moist and tender and has a very luxurious air about it.

Leftovers go fast at my house. Enjoy them at room temperature with fresh, crisp vegetables.

1–2 chicken breasts
¼ cup whole wheat flour
pinch rosemary
pinch thyme
pinch salt
pinch pepper
2 tablespoons butter

Skin the chicken breast, and then bone and cube it. Make a mixture of the flour, spices, salt, and pepper. Dredge the chicken cubes in the flour. Then sauté them in hot melted butter for 3–4 minutes or until the pink juices are gone. Remove to a platter. Serve immediately or keep the chicken warm while you prepare a sauce.

Variation: Lemon Chicken

Once the chicken has been removed to a platter, squeeze a whole lemon into the still-hot pan. If desired, add 1–2 tablespoons white wine and deglaze the pan over medium heat by scraping the bottom of the pan as the sauce bubbles. This should take about 2 minutes. Return the chicken to the pan, stir to coat, heat through, and serve.

RED MEAT

The repertoire of red meat recipes in this chapter demonstrates use of inexpensive and/or low-fat cuts of meat available in small quantities, as well as techniques permitting you to get the best value and satisfaction from that occasional steak, chop, or roast.

The cuts of meat in the chart on p. 120 are small enough to be eaten in one meal. If they are packaged, part of the meat can be frozen for future use. Be sure to watch for meats that have been marked down—there are bargains there!

❧ SELECTING APPROPRIATE CUTS OF MEATS ❧

Cut of Meat	Single Serving Size	Comment
Beef short ribs	¾ pound with bone	Tasty and reasonable, but very high in excess fat. Cut away all but a few thin layers.
Ground chuck	2–3 ounces	Medium-priced ground beef with enough fat to maintain tenderness in cooking. Versatile. Don't overhandle.
Ground lamb	2–3 ounces	Distinct, strong flavor. Excellent with rosemary, mint, yogurt, cilantro.
Ground round	2–3 ounces	Higher-priced ground beef. Lowest fat content. Long cooking can toughen.
Lamb shank	¾–1 pound with bone	Very reasonable. One small shank good for one meal. Cutting meat from bone may be difficult. Braise whole shank, use liquid in cooking.
Liver (beef, calf, veal)	2–3 ounces	Cheap, tasty, tender if not overcooked. Low in fat, good source of iron, protein, A and B vitamins. Must be eaten or frozen within 24 hours of purchase.
Organ meats (tongue, tripe, sweetbreads, heart, kidneys, brain)	2–3 ounces	Excellent protein source, low in fat, varying availability. Recipes not featured here due to price, preparation, or portion-size limitations. Consult family-sized basic cookbook.
Sirloin tips (chunks)	2–3 ounces	Very tender when sautéed. No excess fat, quick cooking.
Stew meat (beef, lamb)	2–3 ounces, trimmed	Requires prolonged cooking for tenderness. Reasonably priced. Strong in flavor. Avoid fat, gristle.
Stew meat (veal)	2–3 ounces	Expensive, very tender, delicate after prolonged cooking. No excess fat.
Teriyaki steak strips	2–3 ounces	Very thin and lean. Medium-to-high priced. Cook hot and fast; stir-fry is best. Flavor with ginger, soy sauce, oyster sauce.
Veal shanks	⅓–½ pound with bones	The cheapest cut of veal, very cheap. Have butcher slice shanks into ½-inch pieces. Extremely tender when braised.

Joe's Special

This concoction appears on many a lunch menu in San Francisco's financial district. It was originated by a man named Peter Arrigoni at a restaurant called New Joe's, and it caught on locally. Despite the use of hamburger, the dish has a lean, high-pro feel to it. It is assembled quickly on top of the stove once the spinach is cooked.

2–3 ounces ground chuck
1 10-ounce package frozen, chopped spinach, cooked and drained
pinch celery salt
pinch pepper
2 eggs, slightly beaten
1 tablespoon grated Parmesan cheese

In a skillet, brown the hamburger. Add the spinach, celery salt, and pepper. Stir to mix. Pour the eggs over the mixture. Cook until it is set, stirring occasionally. Top with Parmesan cheese and serve.

Persian Bulghur & Lamb Casserole

Serve this with plain yogurt and mint tea. Select a pan with a lid that can go into the oven.

½ pound ground lamb
¼ onion, chopped
1 garlic clove, chopped fine
¼ teaspoon rosemary
pinch pepper
⅛ teaspoon salt
2 tomatoes, diced
¾ cup water
½ cup bulghur (cracked wheat)

Preheat the oven to 325° F.
Sauté the lamb and onion over medium-high heat until the meat is brown. Add the remaining ingredients, except the bulghur, and bring to a boil. Add the bulghur and mix.

Cover and bake for 1 hour in the oven. Serve.

Variation

Substitute ground beef for lamb. Flavor with ⅛ teaspoon oregano and use ¼ cup long-grain rice instead of bulghur. Add ¼ cup sautéed green pepper, if desired.

Kefta

An authentic Moroccan recipe for kefta was given to me by my friend and neighbor Pat O'Reilly, who did her tour of Peace Corps duty in Fez. While my adaptation wouldn't pass muster in the casbah, it's nevertheless a pretty good approximation of Moroccan meatballs cooked in sauce. The original recipe has many more steps, and this will take some time as it is!

This recipe freezes nicely, so you may want to triple it and package it for the future. Don't triple the cumin or cayenne, though—just increase them by half.

Enjoy kefta with fresh crusty bread.

¼ **pound lean ground chuck**
2 **tablespoons very finely chopped onion**
1 **tablespoon chili powder**
2 **teaspoons finely chopped parsley**
pinch salt
¼ **teaspoon cumin**
pinch cayenne
1½ **tablespoons olive oil**
1 **tomato, chopped**
¼ **green pepper, chopped fine**
¼ **teaspoon cumin**
pepper to taste
salt to taste
pinch cayenne
1–2 **tablespoons water**
1 **egg**

Thoroughly combine the first seven ingredients and form small meatballs (1 inch in diameter). Set the raw meatballs aside while you make the sauce.

In a deep frying pan, combine all the remaining ingredients, except the egg.

Bring the sauce to a boil. With a large spoon, gently place the meatballs in the sauce so that they aren't touching each other. Reduce the heat to a simmer and cook for 15 minutes, making certain that the meatballs are covered with sauce.

Now here's the authentic part: When the meatballs are cooked, clear a space in the pan and break the egg directly into the sauce. When the egg is poached, your kefta is ready to eat.

Veal Shanks

Also known as Osso Buco, this dish is absolutely delicious, rating four stars for taste, tenderness, and satisfaction (it feels nourishing). Also, it is very cheap. Veal shanks don't cost what the rest of the little veal body costs, probably because of the bone in the center, which is filled with an excellent bonus of marrow.

Ask your butcher to slice the veal shank into ½-inch discs if it is not already done.

Once you've prepared the dish for baking, it must cook for 1½ hours. Can you stand it?

½ yellow onion, diced
½ carrot, cut into small dice
1 tablespoon plus 2 teaspoons olive oil
1 large garlic clove, chopped fine
3–4 teaspoons ½-inch strips of lemon peel, narrow and long
¾ pound sliced veal shanks (3–4 pieces)
3–4 tablespoons unbleached, all-purpose flour
1 cup beef broth
2 tomatoes, chopped
¼ teaspoon basil
¼ teaspoon thyme
pinch pepper
1 bay leaf

Preheat the oven to 350° F.

Select a medium-sized, covered skillet that can go into the oven.

Sauté the onion and carrot in 1 tablespoon oil until the onion is translucent. Add the garlic and lemon peel and continue to cook for 5 minutes. Pour the contents of the pan onto a plate.

Dredge the veal shank pieces in the flour. Heat 2 teaspoons oil in the pan and fry the veal until it is browned. Add ⅓ cup of the broth and scrape the bottom of the pan. Add the tomatoes, sautéed vegetables, basil, thyme, and pepper. Add the remaining ⅔ cup of broth and the bay leaf. Bring to a boil. (If the liquid does not cover the veal, add water.)

Place the mixture in the oven with the lid slightly ajar. Cook for 1½ hours, basting from time to time. The veal shanks are done when the meat has pulled away from the bone and can be easily pierced with a fork.

Stir-Fried Teriyaki Steak

The teriyaki strips are merely thin slices of lean beef. When stir-frying beef with a vegetable, briefly cook the beef, then remove it so the vegetables can cook without toughening the meat. Finally, the beef is returned to the pan to be reheated.

If you don't have a wok, select a sauté pan and fit it with a makeshift lid, or use a skillet with a lid.

2 teaspoons cornstarch
2 teaspoons soy sauce
5–6 lean beef strips
2 tablespoons vegetable oil
¼ teaspoon finely chopped fresh ginger
1 garlic clove, finely chopped
¼ cup beef broth
¼ pound fresh green beans, trimmed

Dissolve the cornstarch in the soy sauce and add the beef strips. Set aside.

Heat the oil over medium-high heat. Add the ginger and garlic and stir briefly. Add the beef mixture, stir to cook, and remove from the pan.

Add the broth and the green beans to the pan. Cover and simmer for 7–8 minutes, or until the beans are al dente. Return the beef to the pan just to heat through. Serve immediately.

Variations

- Beef with broccoli and mushrooms.
- Beef with celery, water chestnuts, and onion wedges.
- Beef with mung bean sprouts and mushrooms.
- Beef with snow peas and green onions in oyster sauce.
- Beef with asparagus and lemon slices (peel included).
- Beef with brussels sprouts and thinly sliced carrot.

Patty's Quick Pâté

This pâté is something you'll want to keep on hand—if not ready-made, then ready-to-make! It's excellent as a snack or as an addition to a main-dish cold plate for lunch or dinner. You can keep it for up to two weeks in the refrigerator.

¼ cup fresh, chopped mushrooms
2 tablespoons plus 2 teaspoons butter (⅓ stick)
3½ ounces liverwurst
1 tablespoon brandy or cognac

Sauté the mushrooms in the butter. Then combine all the ingredients in a blender and whirl to mix well. Turn the mixture into a small container and chill in the refrigerator for a couple of hours. Serve on crackers or French bread.

Baked Short Ribs

This method of preparation may seem austere, but the result is very tasty. Also, this method cooks away some of that pesky fat. Serve accompanied by a generous green salad.

½ **pound short ribs on the bone**
pepper
garlic salt

Preheat the oven to 400° F.

Trim the ribs of excess fat and place them on a cookie sheet. Sprinkle them liberally with pepper and garlic salt. Bake for 15 minutes. Check for doneness then and at 5-minute intervals thereafter. The short ribs are done when the meat is only slightly pink when sliced with a sharp knife.

Bauernschmaus

Bauernschmaus in Germany, choucroute garnie in France, no two versions of this dish are the same. Some recipes call for the apple to cook in the sauerkraut, but here the sauerkraut is heated separately.

Leftovers keep in the refrigerator for up to four days.

1 **whole medium-sized onion, peeled**
1 **whole medium-sized russet or new potato, unpeeled**
1 **whole carrot, scraped, cut in half crosswise**
1 **parsnip, rutabaga, or turnip, optional**
1 **bay leaf**
8–10 **peppercorns**
1 **whole apple, cored, unpeeled**
1 **bockwurst**
½ **cup sauerkraut (fresh or canned)**

Fill a soup pot with water and bring the onion, potato, carrot, parsnip, bay leaf, and peppercorns to a boil. Then, reduce the heat, and cook for 10 minutes over medium–low heat, covered. Add the whole apple and continue cooking. After an additional 20 minutes, reduce the heat to a simmer and add the bockwurst.

In a separate saucepan, heat the sauerkraut. After 10 minutes the bockwurst will be hot and the meal ready to serve. Remove the boiled dinner from the soup pot and arrange with the sauerkraut on a plate (or platter!). Serve with a selection of mustards and horseradish.

Lamb Shank with Lentils

After the lamb has been braised for a bit, lentils are added to the liquid, along with some fresh tomato. The lentils will absorb most of the liquid.

1 tablespoon olive oil
1 garlic clove, minced
¼ teaspoon rosemary
¼ teaspoon oregano
1 tablespoon chopped fresh parsley
1 small lamb shank
2 cups chicken broth
1 bay leaf
¾ cup lentils
1 tomato, diced
½ carrot, chopped fine, optional
pepper
yogurt

Choose a medium-sized skillet with a lid. Heat the olive oil over medium-high heat. Add the garlic, rosemary, oregano, parsley, and the lamb shank. Brown the lamb shank. Add the chicken broth and the bay leaf. Bring to a boil, reduce the heat, and cover. Simmer for 30 minutes.

Add the lentils, tomato, carrot, and pepper to the liquid, cover, and cook for 45 minutes. Serve topped with yogurt.

Pat's Italian Picnic Shoulder

Pat LaGrave, a member of my pre-publication editing team, finds many uses for a small ham. Here's what she offers:

"A single person can get a small shoulder, cook it for company, freeze individual slices, and make a ham salad. You can glaze or top the ham with anything that goes with garlic and won't burn in the oven. It's great, and, of course, you have the ham water and the bone for split pea soup, black beans, or limas. A total win."

1 small picnic shoulder (smoked or plain)
6 garlic cloves
¾ cup white wine vinegar

Remove all the skin from the ham. Quarter the garlic cloves and stick them into the meat. Then add the vinegar to a large kettle and place the ham in it. Cover the ham with water. Simmer for about 20 minutes per pound.

Preheat the oven to 300° F. Remove the ham from the kettle, place it in a baking dish, and bake for 10 minutes per pound. Serve.

Liver and Onions

Don't overcook liver! It cooks very quickly, so it won't be blood rare. Many cooks used to blanch liver before frying it. Don't do that either. Some of the vitamins swim off into oblivion. ♠

⅓ **cup unbleached, all-purpose flour**
⅛ **teaspoon pepper**
⅛ **teaspoon salt**
¼ **teaspoon basil**
2 **tablespoons butter**
1 **small onion, sliced thin**
3 **ounces liver (1 strip)**

Combine the flour with the pepper, salt, and basil.

In a frying pan, melt the butter and sauté the onion until tender—to your taste. Remove the onion to a plate. Retain the butter in the pan.

Dredge the liver in the seasoned flour. Fry over medium heat for 1 minute on each side. Test for doneness by slicing into the center. The meat should be only slightly pink. When done, top with the onion and serve.

Variations

- Sauté the onion with wedges of apple. Season with caraway seeds.
- Serve with strips of cooked bacon.
- Finish the pan juices with 1 tablespoon wine vinegar for a sauce.

Potato Stuffed Sausage

The sausage in this recipe is a very delicate one made from veal. Some brands are treated with nitrites, but many are not, and can be enjoyed without reservation. Don't prick the sausage before heating. ♠

1 **bockwurst**
½ **teaspoon mustard**
1 **small potato, cooked and mashed**
⅛ **teaspoon salt**
2 **tablespoons grated cheddar cheese**
2 **tablespoons milk**

Place the sausage in a pan of cold water. Bring to a boil, then reduce to a quiet simmer for 7 minutes. Then, if you want to, fry the cooked bockwurst slowly in a small amount of oil until it is browned on all sides.

Slit the sausage lengthwise to open, but don't cut it completely in half. Spread the inside with a thin layer of mustard. Combine the mashed potato with the salt, cheese, and milk and heap this mixture onto the open sausage.

If desired, top the potato with additional cheese and broil until it is melted. Serve.

Tagine be Zitun

A tagine is a kind of Moroccan cooking roughly translated as "stew." The original recipe, brought from Morocco by my neighbor, Pat, would have served about twelve people and was made with pieces of shoulder and shank still on the bone. The unusual quality of that recipe will be preserved if the tagine is made with a small lamb shank, since you will get the benefit of the marrow, tendons, and bone, and the pleasure of ferreting morsels of meat from the hollows and crannies of the joint. Another advantage of cooking with the lamb shank is that it is a nice, cheap cut of meat. Lamb stew meat is a perfectly acceptable substitute, however—just reduce the olive oil as listed.

By all means, save the delicious oil from the bottom of the pan! Strain these precious drippings into a freezer container labeled "Lemon Lamb Oil," and use later to sauté vegetables for a soup or stew.

A yogurt and tomato salad is a lovely companion to this dish.

1 small lamb shank (or ⅓ pound lamb stew meat)
¼ cup olive oil (or 2 tablespoons olive oil for stew meat version)
¼ teaspoon ground ginger
pinch saffron, optional
½ medium-sized onion, chopped fine
3 ounces Mediterranean cracked or rose olives, optional
1 small lemon, thinly sliced

Select a heavy, covered pan which is large enough to hold the lamb shank. Prepare the lamb shank for cooking by cutting through the meat to the bone in several places. The shank is protected by a thick shield of connective tissue, and slitting it permits faster cooking. Watch your hands!

Heat the olive oil over medium heat. Add the spices, onion, and olives and reduce the heat to low. Add the lemon and the lamb shank or stew meat, place the lid on the pan, and cook for a half-hour, basting the meat from time to time as it cooks. A test of doneness is whether the meat comes easily away from the bone.

FISH
&
SHELLFISH

People tell me they rarely prepare fish for themselves—usually because they are uncertain about what to buy and how to proceed. I want this chapter to clear up any questions or confusion, because I think fish is one of the most valuable contributions to the human diet. In fact, I subscribe to the notion that fish is brain food. It is high in protein, very low in fat, and contains a wealth of minerals and trace nutrients. Those of us living near the water can usually get fish fresh in any quantity, including single filets. But there is also a good selection of frozen fish and shellfish for those of you in areas less blessed. Review the recipes and tips I have provided and experiment with the types of fish available to you.

The first section of this chapter deals with fish and the second section is concerned with shellfish.

Buying Fish

If you buy whole fish, save yourself some trouble and make certain the butcher cleans it for you. It can be a rude surprise to have your mind on baked pompano, only to discover that a slimy misadventure lies between you and the *pièce de résistance*.

A key consideration in your decision to buy fish whole is whether you want to be concerned with the bones. When you filet the fish (usually after it is cooked), you cannot be certain you have all the bones. Because of this problem, I buy whole fish only when I am clear of mind and full of patience.

Fish filets are an excellent way to buy fish. Fresh or thawed, filets are ready to cook, and there are no preparation techniques not easily mastered. If you buy a fresh filet in a package, read the label to determine whether it has ever been frozen. If so, it should say "Fresh-Frozen," and the fish may be a little bland and just slightly waterlogged.

If you buy filets frozen, keep them that way until you plan to use them. You may even cook the fish frozen, but allow an additional few minutes of cooking time. Raw fish cannot be refrozen once it has been thawed. Cooked fish can be frozen and then baked in a 350° F. oven when you are ready to serve it. The length of baking time depends on the fish.

Cooking Fish

The most important thing to remember about cooking fish is that it becomes tough when overcooked. Many types of fish have a translucence which disappears as the fish cooks. Once the flesh is opaque, the fish is done.

Salmon and swordfish are denser-fleshed fish and must be kept moist as they cook. Often they are basted in clarified butter. A test for doneness is whether the flesh can be separated into flakes with a fork. Of course, overdone fish will flake, also.

Poached Red Snapper

To poach any fish it is first desirable to make a court bouillon. This delicately flavored liquid is the classic means of poaching fish without overpowering it. Select as many red snapper filets as you will want, and have them ready to poach once the court bouillon comes to a boil.

3–4 peppercorns
1 bay leaf
2 celery ribs (including leaves)
6–8 thin slices of carrot
¼ cup vinegar
3–4 onion slices
1–2 fresh parsley sprigs
½ teaspoon salt
1–2 fish filets

Fill a skillet with 1½–2 inches of water and add all of the ingredients except the fish. Bring this floating garden to a boil, and then reduce the heat.

Immerse the red snapper filets in the court bouillon and poach them until the translucency of the fish is gone and the fish is tender but not too flaky when pierced with a fork. Remove the fish from the pan with a slotted spatula and allow it to drain before serving.

Curried Butterfish

This dish is bright yellow. Butterfish was selected because it doesn't usually come to mind with curry, and I want to demonstrate the great flexibility you have in your fish choices. Buy any white fish that's in season or on sale, knowing that it will make for a fine dinner.

Here you will use the familiar Indian technique of adding the spices to melted butter, which brings the curry to life. The fish is then bathed in this mixture and cooked over high heat.

Select a frying pan with a sturdy handle since you'll be shaking the pan from time to time to rotate the fish strips.

1 tablespoon butter
1 tablespoon minced onion
½ teaspoon curry powder
1–2 fish filets

Melt the butter in a frying pan. Once the butter has begun to melt, add the onion and sauté until it begins to turn translucent. Then add the curry powder and blend it thoroughly with the butter. Cut the fish filet lengthwise into ½-inch strips and place them in the frying pan. Shake the pan gently, or turn the fish pieces with a big wooden spoon, making certain that the pieces are coated with the curry. The fish will cook very quickly, and you will see the clear fish flesh turn white almost immediately. As it cooks, shake the pan from time to time so that all sides cook evenly. You don't want the fish to break as you do this. Once the fish flakes easily and the flakes are white in the center as well as on the outside, after 4–5 minutes of cooking, remove it to your plate and top with fresh lemon juice, or the rich but quick Savory Lemon and Cream Sauce, p. 184.

Fish Stew with Fennel

Fresh fennel contributes a wonderfully fragrant bouquet with a slight anise flavor to this recipe. You may use any fresh or fresh-frozen filet of a white-fleshed fish. I prefer to use cod. The proportions should provide you with one hearty serving, but you may double the recipe. You'll want more!

Eat any leftovers within two days.

2 tablespoons butter
¼ onion, chopped
½ cup chicken broth
¼ cup white wine
½ potato, diced
¼ teaspoon fennel seed, crushed
1 fish filet, cut up

Melt the butter in a soup pot and sauté the onion. Add the chicken broth and white wine and bring the mixture to a boil. Then add the potato and fennel and reduce the heat to a simmer until the potato is tender—about 8 minutes. Finally, add the pieces of fish and simmer for about 5 minutes. Serve.

Quick Fish Stew

This takes just minutes to cook, and the tomatoes and pepper give it a garden-fresh quality. I've kept the ingredients simple, but don't hesitate to create your own combinations. It really does well with fresh herbs. Tarragon, oregano, basil, and, of course, parsley have all been very successful. Use just a leaf or two, minced.

Eat leftover fish stew within two days.

1 tablespoon olive oil
1 garlic clove, minced
½ onion, chopped
½ green pepper, chopped
2 tomatoes, chopped
½ cup tomato sauce
½ cup water
2 teaspoons lemon juice
1½ teaspoons soy sauce
¾ pound fresh fish filets, cut in chunks
½ teaspoon fresh herbs

In a saucepan, heat the oil and sauté the garlic, onion, and green pepper, just until the onion is limp. Combine the tomatoes, tomato sauce, water, lemon juice, and soy sauce with the sautéed ingredients. Bring to a boil and let boil for 5 minutes. Add the fish pieces and fresh herbs, and reduce the heat to a simmer. Simmer for about 8 minutes, or until the fish flakes easily. Serve.

Quenelles

This recipe is one of the simpler versions of quenelles. Quenelles are light fish dumplings, delicate and tasty. Since they tend to be a little rich, it's a good idea to save half the mixture to be eaten later in the week.

Pike is the traditional choice for quenelles, although any white-fleshed fish will be good.

The batter keeps for two days in the refrigerator, but once made, the quenelles must be eaten promptly.

¼ pound pike
⅛ teaspoon salt
1 egg white
pinch white pepper
1 ice cube, cracked
½ cup heavy cream
¼ teaspoon dill weed

Cut the pike into strips and place it in your blender jar along with the salt. Blend it in pulses until the fish is a paste, about 15 seconds. Then add the egg white, the pinch of white pepper, and the ice cube and blend again until mixed, about 10 more seconds. Gradually add the heavy cream. Once the cream has been added, the consistency should be smooth and quite thick.

In a large frying pan, bring 1½ inches of salted water to a simmer. Form the quenelles by buttering a soup spoon and forming a smooth ball with the fish mixture. Gently slip each quenelle into the simmering water and cook for 10 minutes, rolling each one over gently after 5 minutes. Remove them carefully with a slotted spoon and place them on your serving plate. Serve topped with the dill weed, and Poached Fish Sauce (p. 184), if desired.

SALMON

My memory of the best salmon I ever ate is when my grandparents drove me to Bodega Bay on one of my college breaks. My grandmother, the tireless hostess of many family gatherings, had devised a menu which was perfect for this al fresco meal. We stopped at the local fish market and bought salmon steaks. Then my grandfather cooked them in a cast-iron skillet, using plenty of butter, over an open fire on the beach. The salmon skin was crispy, the flesh pink and flaky, and there was just a hint of a marvelous smoky flavor. We ate on paper plates in the brisk Pacific Ocean wind, and it couldn't have tasted better.

For single portions, a fresh salmon steak is just right. The steak should be about ½ inch thick. Eat it the same day you buy it to really savor the freshness.

Frying. Butter is the best oil for frying, but it must not burn. Get your frying pan medium-hot, and add the butter to it. Let it melt, and then add the salmon steak. Cook it for about 4 minutes to a side, and check for doneness by seeing if the center bone moves readily away from the flesh. Also, the pink flesh should be increasingly flaky as it cooks—flaky, but *not* dry.

Once the salmon steak is cooked and removed to a platter, you may quickly make a sauce from the pan juices by adding some lemon juice, dry vermouth or white wine, and, at the last minute, capers. Quickly drizzle the sauce over your salmon steak, and it will be ready to eat.

Broiling. This method is effective if you don't let the fish dry out. Make sure the broiler is quite hot (preheat for about 7 minutes). Place the salmon steak about 5 inches down from the heat source. It should broil for 5 minutes on the first side, and 7 minutes or so on the second side. Baste at regular intervals of about 1 minute, using clarified butter. (Clarified butter is used because it will not burn during broiling.) You may test for doneness by gently flaking the salmon with a fork. The flaked fish should have lost most of its translucence in the center, and the bone in the center of the filet should lift out easily.

Baking. This method works well if you wrap the fish in foil. Preheat the oven to 350° F., then bake the sealed fish for about 25 minutes. While the salmon steak is baking, you can make Hollandaise Sauce (p. 178), although a mixture of a little butter, lemon, and fresh pepper is less trouble, less fattening, and quite tasty.

Barbecuing. A marinade is in order here to prevent the salmon from drying out. Make a simple mixture of 3 tablespoons olive oil, 1 tablespoon lemon juice, 1 teaspoon tomato paste, and ½ teaspoon dill weed. Once the coals are hot, the salmon steak will require 8 minutes of cooking. Brush it regularly with the marinade and turn after 4 minutes. Test for doneness by checking for flaking and by jiggling the center bone to see if it moves freely away from the flesh.

Salmon Salad

1 PORTION

This salad is delicious on a bed of greens with tomatoes and quartered eggs, or as a sandwich spread. The salmon is so moist that very little dressing is needed.

Any leftover poached or baked fish can be used for this tasty salad.

½ cup cooked salmon
1 tablespoon finely chopped green pepper
1 tablespoon chopped green onion
2 teaspoons chopped parsley
2 tablespoons finely chopped celery
mayonnaise or sour cream to moisten

Combine all ingredients in a bowl and mix. You can also add radish slivers, capers, and chopped black olives, if you wish.

Salmon Patty

This dish works well with canned salmon. You may eat the patty plain with lemon juice, or it can be featured in a much more elaborate dish. For instance, picture it in a ring of zucchini discs alternated with thinly sliced, oven-browned potatoes and garnished with sour cream and parsley. Or, how about heaping some shredded lettuce and tartar sauce on a French roll and setting the salmon patty on top?

⅓ cup canned salmon, or leftover poached or baked salmon
1 egg, slightly beaten
1 tablespoon whole wheat flour
1 teaspoon dill weed
2 teaspoons lemon juice
½ teaspoon pepper
1 tablespoon minced onion
1 tablespoon vegetable oil

Blend all of the ingredients except the oil and form the mixture into a patty, taking care not to over-handle it. Fry it in the oil over very low heat, turning the patty after about 7 minutes. Cook the second side for 5 minutes, then serve.

Salmon Casserole with Potato

This one-dish meal is reminiscent of Shepherd's Pie (p. 117). Leave the skin on the potato for extra nutrition.

½ potato, diced
2 tablespoons butter
1 tablespoon chopped onion
2 tablespoons chopped mushrooms
½ teaspoon lemon juice
½ teaspoon oregano
½ can salmon (6½-ounce size)
3 tablespoons half-and-half or milk
3 tablespoons grated Swiss cheese

Preheat the oven to 350° F.

Cook the potato in a small saucepan in about ⅛ inch of boiling water and a pinch of salt.

In a small skillet, melt 1 tablespoon of the butter, and sauté the onion and mushrooms. Then add the lemon juice and oregano and stir. Add the salmon and allow it to heat through.

When the potato is tender, mash it with the remaining 1 tablespoon of butter, half-and-half, and Swiss cheese.

In a greased individual casserole dish, place ⅓ of the mashed potatoes. Then add the salmon mixture. Top with the remaining mashed potatoes. Bake for 20–25 minutes. Serve.

Broiled Catfish

Like most fish, this one is successfully served with lemon. You can make a quick tartar sauce by mixing some pickle relish with mayonnaise.

Buy one whole, cleaned catfish, unattractive as it may be....

Preheat your broiler. Baste the catfish with butter both inside and out. Cover your broiling pan with foil and place the catfish on the foil about 3 inches below the flame or element of the broiler. Broil one side of a 9-inch catfish for 8 minutes, then turn and broil the other side for 6 minutes.

Place the fish on a platter. To filet the cooked fish, you'll need first to make a cut along the fish's backbone. Then, with the tines of a fork, pry the top filet off the bone by lifting gently from the backbone upward in several places. The meat will come away from the bone fairly easily. Once the top filet is free, set it aside on the platter and simply lift the now-exposed skeleton off the bottom half of the fish. Catfish is one of the easiest fish to filet because of the firm flesh and large bones.

Ceviche

In this Mexican recipe (pronounced seh vee' chay) the fish is "cooked" through marination. Immerse fish pieces in lemon/lime juice in the morning, and the ceviche is ready to eat in the afternoon or evening. The fish should be marinated in the refrigerator for a minimum of 5 hours. A pie pan is perfect for marinating, since a flat surface allows the whole fish to mix with the juice.

1 fish filet, chopped
raw shrimp or scallops, optional
juice of 2 lemons or 1 lemon and 1 lime
1 tomato, chopped
1 teaspoon chopped cilantro
chopped green onion or sliced onion ring
1 garlic clove, sliced, optional
2 tablespoons chopped red or green pepper, optional
1 tablespoon chopped pimiento, optional

Combine the ingredients in a pie pan or other flat-bottomed dish.

If you are around while the ceviche is marinating, you should stir it from time to time to insure total exposure to the lemon/lime juice. If you have to be away and won't be able to turn the fish, add enough juice to completely cover it.

Once the ceviche has marinated (the fish will no longer be translucent), it can be garnished with a wedge of lemon and served on a salad plate.

Fish Pudding

Forgive the dull title. This recipe is a poor relation to the elegant soufflé. I have given a plain name to a good, plain dish.

To prepare the fish, a food mill with a medium-sized blade works well. The goal is to give the fish, mushroom, and egg mixture a very fine consistency.

Generously oil one 5–6-inch soufflé dish, or four individual custard cups. Once the pudding is ready to bake, you may store it in the refrigerator for two days before baking.

2 tablespoons butter
3–4 mushrooms, sliced
½ cup milk
1 slice whole wheat toast, crumbled
⅜ cup canned fish
1 egg, beaten

Preheat the oven to 400° F.

In a saucepan, melt the butter and sauté the mushrooms. Once sautéed, remove the mushrooms with a slotted spoon and put them aside, leaving the butter in the pan. To the saucepan, add the milk and crumbled toast. Simmer for about 10 minutes while you prepare the fish.

Chop the sautéed mushrooms and combine them with the fish and the beaten egg. Then chop the mixture in a food mill or process in a blender with 3 tablespoons of the milk mixture until smooth. Remove the milk mixture from the heat and allow it to cool slightly.

Combine the fish and milk mixtures and pour into a greased soufflé dish or individual custard cups. Bake until a knife comes out clean when the center of the pudding is pierced—30–45 minutes depending on the size of the dish. Serve.

Trout Meunière

Use a whole trout, including head, tail, and scaly skin, and don't forget that it will still have all its bones. If you are reluctant to look the fish in the eye, or if you are worried that you won't be able to filet the fish thoroughly, you can substitute a filet of sole instead. The recipe will work just as well.

Trout Meunière is a fried-fish dish, but the fish is first soaked in milk, then dredged in flour to form a delicate casing to contain the moisture and flavor. You'll need a skillet wide enough to hold the whole fish.

⅓ cup milk
1 whole trout
3 tablespoons unbleached, all-
  purpose flour
pinch salt
pinch pepper
1 tablespoon vegetable oil
1 tablespoon butter
juice of ½ lemon

Pour the milk into a loaf pan and put the fish in the milk. Allow it to sit for about half an hour, rotating it occasionally. Combine the flour, salt, and pepper. Put the flour mixture on a dinner plate. Remove the milky fish to the flour mixture and coat the fish top and bottom.

Add the oil to the skillet and warm it to medium-hot. Then add the butter and allow it to melt completely. Once the butter is hot, but not burned, add the trout. Fry it for about 3 minutes to a side. When the trout is done (flaky inside), transfer it to your dinner plate and squeeze the lemon over it. Top with more butter if you like.

SHELLFISH

This section is small but essential. Small, because shellfish is both expensive and unavailable to many people, especially in the interior areas. Essential, because shellfish provide some of the finest tastes the palate can savor.

Some Cleaning Guidelines

Shrimp and prawns should be rinsed thoroughly under cold water. Once cooked and cooled you may want to devein them. Remove the shell and, holding the shrimp under cold running water, use your thumbnail to take out the dark vein running the length of the shrimp's back.

Clams and mussels should be rinsed under cold water. Those that clamp shut are okay. Discard any opened clams or mussels and also any unusually heavy ones—they are probably filled with sand.

Crab cleaning is a rather elaborate process which has more to do with removal of the inedible portions than with "washing." Have your butcher do it!

Basic Sauces

You will be far more flexible in your approach to shellfish preparation if you bear in mind some rudiments, and then improvise. A very simple sauce can be started by sautéing the shellfish in garlic and butter. A little white wine or clam juice can extend this base, and the sauce can be thickened with a teaspoon of cornstarch (dissolved in cold water first).

Another direction to take is the Marinara Seafood Sauce, p. 183.

Prawns in Lemon Butter

1 PORTION

You'll want a good, crusty bread to eat with this dish. I would choose a French roll or a hard roll. No silverware is needed. The prawns are baked in an ovenproof dish with a lid.

¼ **pound raw prawns or shrimp**
⅓ **stick butter, sliced**
½ **lemon, sliced thin**
1 **teaspoon pepper**

Preheat the oven to 375° F.

Layer the prawns in a casserole dish with the sliced butter and lemon. Sprinkle with the fresh pepper. Put a lid on the dish and bake for 25 minutes.

When the prawns (or shrimp) are a nice pink color, they're done. They're also extremely hot. Trans-fer them to a dinner plate and allow them to cool enough to eat. You'll have to peel away the shells with your bare fingers. Serve as soon as you can, and soak up the butter with that wonderful bread.

Variation

My landlady reports: "Prawns grilled on a skewer over mesquite with fresh rosemary on the coals is to die and go to heaven. Garlic butter is the baste. They truly were the best I ever had."

Pete's Prawns Picado

This is just about the fastest of all the shellfish dishes. You decide if it's the best, too.

2 tablespoons vegetable oil
1 garlic clove, minced
½ green pepper, sliced into strips
¼ onion, cut into ⅛-inch slices
1 tomato, quartered
¼ cup water
dash oregano
dash sage
dash thyme
dash cumin
8 fresh or thawed jumbo prawns

In a skillet, heat the oil and garlic and add the green pepper and onion. Stir until the onion becomes translucent. Then add the tomato and water, and simmer for about 10 minutes. Add the spices and continue to cook for 5 more minutes. Add the prawns, cover, and simmer for 3–4 minutes. Check the prawns from time to time. When the flesh is a nice bright pink and has lost its translucency, the dish is done.

Pasta with Clam Sauce

Little Joe's restaurant in San Francisco makes the best pasta with clam sauce I have ever tasted. This recipe was inspired by it.

To save steps here, canned whole clams can be used. The clam juice can be drained from the canned clams and supplemented with bottled clam juice. Should you be so fortunate as to have fresh clams at your disposal, 6–8 cleaned clams will be about right. Steam them until the shells open, shell them, and proceed as instructed.

You can make the sauce while the pasta is cooking.

6 quarts water, salted
1 cup pasta, uncooked
1 tablespoon butter
1 garlic clove
⅓ cup shelled clams
½ cup clam juice
2 tablespoons chopped fresh parsley
⅛ teaspoon oregano
butter
salt
pepper

Bring about 6 quarts of salted water to a rolling boil. Add the pasta and stir to be certain it isn't clumping. Continue to stir periodically as it cooks.

Melt 1 tablespoon butter in a sauté pan and add the garlic. Sauté to flavor the butter, about 30 seconds, then remove and discard the garlic. Add the clams and the clam juice and heat thoroughly. Add the parsley and the oregano and remove from the heat.

Drain the pasta and toss lightly with the butter, salt, and pepper. Top the pasta with the clam sauce and garnish with more fresh parsley. Mangia, Mangia!

Oyster Stew

My initiation to oyster stew came while I was reading The Art of Eating by M.F.K. Fisher. Her rhapsodic description of its delicacy and richness was so inviting that I put the book down and went to the store and bought a pint of oysters and a pint of heavy cream. I came home and made a stew as tender and creamy as she promised it would be. I ate the whole dish in one sitting, savoring every bite. You'll note I've taken some liberties with this recipe. However, the substitution of half-and-half for heavy cream (a concession to our national need to reduce fat intake) still produces a delectable stew.

Oysters are usually available in the meat market in pint jars of one dozen oysters. Leave the extra oysters in the jar with juice covering them and keep them refrigerated. Use them within two days by making more stew, or by making baked oysters (see Variation). ❧

¾ cup clam juice
4–5 fresh, raw oysters
¾ cup half-and-half
1 tablespoon butter

In a saucepan bring half the clam juice to a boil; then reduce the heat to a simmer. Add the raw oysters and cook them for 2½ to 3 minutes. In another pan, heat the half-and-half, butter, and remaining clam juice. Remove the oysters with a slotted spoon and add them to the half-and-half. Then serve.

Variation: Baked Oysters

Baking is a perfect way to gently cook oysters. Preheat the oven to 450° F. Generously butter an individual casserole dish. Add 5 or 6 oysters and top with 2–3 tablespoons of oyster juice or white wine. Bake for 10 minutes or until the oysters are plump and their edges are curled.

Oysters can also be eaten raw, of course. My father throws them down with reckless abandon, shucking them and eating them right on the beach.

Mussels with Risotto

I grew up on Puget Sound in Washington State and had as much shellfish as I could ever want—or so I thought. Yet I (and my family and friends) overlooked one of the tastiest and most abundant types of shellfish to be found in the Puget Sound. I'm still kicking myself for all the years I spent stepping over mussels. Colonies of them clinging to every piling and pier went unnoticed as we gobbled down oysters, crab, and clams. Finally, at a Foire de Gastronomie in Dijon, France, I ordered a bowl of "moules." For about $1.75 I got a couple of dozen fresh mussels in the shell, freshly steamed in white wine, garlic, and sea salt. Quelle révélation! I now make it a point always to sample the bounty of the regions I visit. I'm never sorry.

1 tablespoon butter
2 teaspoons chopped onion
¼ cup long-grain brown rice
½ cup chicken broth
2 tablespoons olive oil
1 small garlic clove, chopped
2 tablespoons white wine or water
6–8 fresh mussels, cleaned

Melt the butter in the bottom of a small pot and sauté the onion in it. Add the rice and heat it briefly in the butter. Then add enough broth just to cover. As it is absorbed, add more broth to cover. Continue this until you have added all the broth.

As the risotto completes cooking, heat the olive oil in a pot or deep skillet. Add the garlic and permit it to flavor the oil. Then add the wine or water (before the garlic browns) and heat. Finally, add the whole mussels. Reduce the heat and put a lid on the pan.

Continue to check the mussels. Once the shells are all opened, turn off the heat and allow the mussels to cool before removing them from their shells. When they are shucked, return them to the garlic/oil liquor. As the risotto becomes tender, add the mussel mixture to it and heat through before devouring.

(To take a shortcut, steam the rice all at once. The risotto won't be quite as creamy, but the flavor will be the same.)

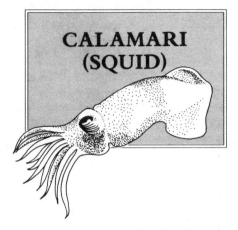

CALAMARI (SQUID)

Squid is one of the best fresh seafood bargains I have found. When purchased frozen, you often have to buy more than you could ever use, and they may be packed so tightly that you have to thaw the whole quantity in order to use a few. But at the fish market you can buy only as many as you want, and the price compares very, very favorably to most other fresh seafood. So, heigh thee to a fishmonger and get ye a handful of squiggly squid!

Cleaning Squid

I'll be frank: Cleaning squid can be unpleasant for the squeamish. But if you're organized and matter-of-fact about it, it won't be a barrier to the pleasures that lie beyond. Work close to your sink, as plenty of cold water is necessary throughout.

1. Have two bowls on hand: one for discards and one for the cleaned squid.

2. Wash the squid's exterior, rubbing off the pink, mottled layer of skin. The squid should be creamy smooth when you've finished.

3. Cut off the head below the eyes, then cut off the tentacles. Rinse the tentacles thoroughly, removing any bits of skin residue or cartilage, and place them in the cleaned-squid bowl. Discard the top of the head.

4. Clean out the squid body, dumping the intestines directly into the discard bowl. There is a piece of cartilage in the body that looks for all the world like a clear plastic insert. Pull it out and discard it also.

5. Give the squid a final rinse, then place it in the cleaned-squid bowl.

6. Slice the squid body into ⅛-inch rings—*unless* you want to stuff it (p. 146).

Now that you have a bowl of cleaned squid, including the tentacles and the squid cut into rings, you can sauté it in a variety of ways. The most common (and successful) method is to melt 3 tablespoons of butter and sauté a sliced clove of garlic. Add the rings and tentacles of 4 squid (1 portion) and sauté until the flesh turns from translucent to white. This takes about 45 seconds!! Enjoy!

A second, very popular way to use squid is in a bouillabaise or other type of fresh fish or shellfish stew. The Quick Fish Stew on p. 134 can be made with squid with excellent results.

Stuffed Squid

This recipe calls for four squid, which make one generous serving. However, the recipe is flexible. Clean as many squid as you intend to use and reserve the tentacles (see p. 145). You'll want the stuffing to be ready to eat before you stuff the squid, because the squid itself will take only moments to cook. I have chosen a light, bread-based stuffing moistened with clam juice and sautéed chopped mushrooms. The squid will be steamed in a garlic/ clam juice base until it is firm and the stuffing is warm.

Choose a sauté pan that is large enough to hold four stuffed squid.

1 tablespoon butter
1 garlic clove
4–5 mushrooms, chopped
4 tentacle sets, chopped
¼ cup clam juice
dash white wine
1 slice whole wheat bread
2 teaspoons chopped fresh parsley
4 squid, cleaned, tentacles removed
1 teaspoon butter
½ cup clam juice

Melt 1 tablespoon butter in a sauté pan. Add the garlic clove and sauté for 30 seconds. Remove the garlic. Sauté the mushrooms and tentacles. Then add just a splash each of the clam juice and the white wine. The rest of the clam juice will be added later. Put a lid on the pan and steam for 2–3 minutes, until the translucent flesh of the tentacles has turned white. Remove from the pan.

Tear the bread into small pieces and toss with the mushrooms, tentacles, and parsley. Pour the remainder of the ¼ cup clam juice into the sauté pan with any remaining butter. Heat, then pour over the stuffing and toss to moisten. Divide the mixture into quarters and stuff each squid.

Add about 1 teaspoon butter and ½ cup clam juice to the pan and bring to a boil. Add the stuffed squid and reduce the heat to a simmer. Check after 5–6 minutes. The squid should be taut and pink. Remove the squid with a slotted spoon and place them on your dinner plate. Serve.

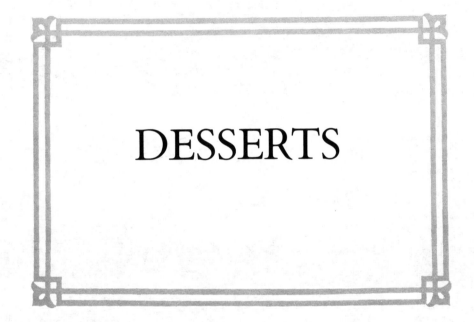

DESSERTS

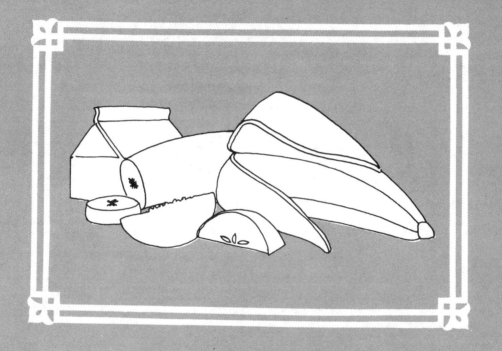

A dessert is a graceful way to end a memorable meal, and that is the spirit in which these recipes are offered. Simple fruit dishes are prominently mentioned because they are so wonderfully suited to this purpose. There are recipes ranging from plain puddings to somewhat more complicated concoctions—tarts, cobblers, betties, and such. From this selection you will quickly discover that the recipe is only a guide. Your own imagination is an even better resource.

Most desserts in this chapter can be made with ingredients at hand; fresh fruit, flour, butter, eggs, milk, nuts, jam, and fruit juice can produce an infinite array of goodies. Invest in some semi-sweet chocolate and perhaps a bottle of rum, and you'll be set.

Sautéed Apple Rings

Firm winter apples are sliced into rings, cored neatly, and gently sautéed until tender in butter, honey, lemon, and spices. This dish is very quickly prepared. The slices are done in about 7 minutes.

1 medium-sized apple or 2 small apples
juice of ½ lemon
1½ tablespoons butter
¼ teaspoon allspice, or ⅛ teaspoon cinnamon or nutmeg
1 teaspoon honey

Core the apple and cut it into ¼-inch slices. Squeeze the lemon juice onto the apple slices to prevent browning. Melt the butter in a sauté pan and add the spice and apples to it. Sauté one side of the apple rings for about 2 minutes, then turn gently and continue to sauté over low heat for an additional 2–3 minutes.

Just before the apples finish cooking (they will be tender but will still hold their shape), drizzle the honey over the apple rings and gently agitate the pan by shaking it back and forth away from you.

Remove the pan from the burner and allow the apple rings to cool somewhat before serving. The honey gets quite hot when it is cooked.

Applesauce I

Forget about the applesauce you buy in cans or jars at the market. Homemade applesauce sets a new and higher standard. It takes only about 10 minutes to make, and the freedom you have to experiment with spices and textures can make each batch unique. Choose a good cooking apple: Pippin, Granny Smith, gravenstein, Rome beauty, McIntosh, and Jonathan are a few you might try.

Leftovers may be kept refrigerated for four days, or may be frozen for later use.

2 cooking apples, quartered, cored, and peeled
2 tablespoons water
1 tablespoon lemon or other citrus juice
2 tablespoons brown sugar, firmly packed
⅛ teaspoon cardamom
⅛ teaspoon nutmeg
2 tablespoons raisins or currants

In a saucepan with a lid, combine the apples, water, lemon juice, and sugar. Simmer with a lid on the pot until the apples have softened, about 5 minutes. Mash the apples to the desired consistency. Add the spices and raisins to the pot and stir to mix. Return the lid to the pot and turn off the heat. Let the applesauce sit while the raisins plump. It will be ready to eat in about 10 minutes.

Applesauce II

This version is just as easy to make as Applesauce I (above)—and it's nuttier. Try it for breakfast, topped with milk or cream.

Leftovers may be refrigerated for four days or frozen for later use.

2 cooking apples, quartered, cored, and peeled
3 tablespoons water
1 tablespoon lemon or other citrus juice
1 tablespoon honey
½ teaspoon allspice
2 tablespoons untoasted wheat germ
2 tablespoons chopped walnuts

In a saucepan with a lid, combine the apples, water, lemon juice, and honey. Simmer with a lid on the pot until the apples have softened. Mash the apples to the desired consistency. Add the spice, wheat germ, and walnuts and stir to mix. Continue to cook for 2–3 minutes. Cool and serve.

Banana Anna

Talk about sweet! A rich apricot sauce envelopes the banana as it bakes in foil.

3 tablespoons apricot jam
¼ teaspoon vanilla
1 tablespoon rum, white wine, or the liqueur of your choice, optional
1 firm, ripe banana

Preheat the oven to 425° F.

In a small saucepan, heat the jam and add the vanilla (and liquor, if desired). Stir until well mixed.

Place the peeled banana in a piece of aluminum foil which is longer than the banana. Fold the foil in half over the banana and crinkle the ends of the foil to form a boat. Pour the sauce into the boat to cover the banana; then seal the foil by folding it twice.

Place the sealed envelope in a cake or pie pan and bake for 15 minutes. When the banana is done, unwrap the foil envelope, slide the banana onto your dessert plate, and serve.

Baked Nectarine

1 PORTION

This is just what a dessert should be—sweet and simple. When nectarines or peaches are fresh during the summer and fall, this dish is an appropriate accompaniment to any meal. Sunday brunch with French toast, a luncheon frittata, or a hearty evening salad all make good companions for a baked nectarine.

1 teaspoon brown sugar
2 teaspoons butter
1 firm, ripe nectarine or peach, washed and halved
yogurt or sour cream, optional

Preheat the oven to 350° F.

Combine the brown sugar and butter. Then divide the mixture and place half in the center of each piece of fruit. Place the nectarine cut-side up in a cake or pie pan and cover the bottom of the pan with ⅛ inch of water. Bake for 20 minutes. Cool slightly before eating. Top with yogurt or sour cream, if desired.

Variation: Curried Nectarine

Midway through baking lightly sprinkle ⅛ teaspoon curry powder over the nectarines (a pinch each). Baste with the pan juice and continue baking.

Brown Betty

This dish may have originated elsewhere, but it has become firmly American. It is a simple fruit pudding bound with breadcrumbs. The pudding bakes first with a lid, then completes baking without, and is served warm with Lemon Sauce.

1 cup peeled, sliced, and cored or pitted apple, peach, or apricot
juice of ½ lemon, and gratings from the rind
1 tablespoon brown sugar
¼ teaspoon cinnamon
⅓ cup breadcrumbs
2 tablespoons butter, melted
¼ cup water
Lemon Sauce (p. 176)

Preheat the oven to 350° F.

Grease an individual casserole dish with a 1½-cup capacity. In a mixing bowl, combine the sliced fruit with the lemon juice, rind gratings, sugar, and cinnamon. In a separate bowl, combine the breadcrumbs and melted butter.

In the casserole dish, layer the fruit and crumb mixtures, finishing with a layer of crumbs. Add ¼ cup water to the dish and bake covered with foil for 20 minutes. Then uncover and bake an additional 15 minutes. Serve topped with warm Lemon Sauce.

Baked Stuffed Pear

Pears respond beautifully to honey, nuts, and butter. Two ripe pear halves form a cradle for the stuffing.

1 tablespoon butter, softened
1 tablespoon finely chopped walnuts or pecans
1 tablespoon honey
1 firm, ripe pear, unpeeled, cored, and halved
yogurt or sour cream, optional

Preheat the oven to 350° F.

Make a mixture of the butter, nuts, and honey and spoon it into the pears. Place the pears cut-side up in a pie or cake pan and add about ⅛ inch of water to the bottom of the pan. Bake for about 30 minutes. Cool slightly before serving. Top with yogurt or sour cream, if desired.

Berry Pudding

This dish is fun to make at the height of summer when you have your pick of fresh berries, but it's also a hit in the wintertime when you can take only the berries you need from a bag in the freezer. Any berry will be good with this recipe. If you choose blueberries, mash them slightly first.

The mixture rises somewhat during baking, so make sure there is room for expansion in your baking dish. An individual casserole dish with a 2-cup capacity should be fine. Butter it for baking.

¼ cup brown sugar, packed
2 tablespoons butter
⅓ cup whole wheat flour
½ teaspoon baking powder
⅛ teaspoon salt
⅓ cup milk
½ cup berries, unsweetened

Preheat the oven to 350° F.

In a medium-sized mixing bowl, combine the brown sugar with the butter. Add the flour, baking powder, salt, and milk and stir until smooth.

Turn the mixture into the buttered casserole dish and top with the berries. Bake for 40 minutes. Cool and serve plain.

❧ CHEESE AS DESSERT ❧

Cheese is an excellent dessert choice, especially when eaten with ripe fruit and perhaps a glass of chilled white wine. The person dining alone needn't buy a wheel of cheese—many cheese shops and delis will happily sell small quantities of cheese to accommodate the sampler. Seek out those stores and experiment with new cheeses. Usually you get a free taste before you buy, so take advantage of this opportunity to discover new tastes.

Below are a few cheeses which I recommend highly. The list is quite incomplete and is in no way representative of all that is available. Bring cheese to room temperature before serving.

Bel Paese
Brie
Camembert
Chèvre
Explorateur
Forme
   d'Ambert
Gorgonzola

Liverot
Mascarpone
Montrachet
Pont L'Eveque
St. André
Stilton
Torta di Gorgonzola e Mascarpone

Pear Belle Hélène

This dish is intended for those occasions when your sweet tooth is going wild. Chocolate, ice cream, and pears make a very successful team—rich, subtle, and sweet. The pears must be poached a day ahead of time. Poach enough pears for another, saner, dessert or salad within the next day or two. Or you can use canned pears and simply skip the poaching step.

2 cups water
1 cup granulated sugar
1 teaspoon vanilla
1 pear, still somewhat firm, peeled, cored, and halved
1 ounce dark sweet chocolate (1 square)
¼ cup whipping cream
vanilla ice cream

In a medium-sized saucepan, bring the water, sugar, and vanilla to a boil and stir to dissolve the sugar. Add the pear, reduce the heat, and simmer for 30 minutes, or until the pear halves are tender. Cool the poached pear to room temperature, then refrigerate for 24 hours.

On the day of the feast, melt the chocolate over medium heat in a heavy saucepan. Briskly stir in the whipping cream with a coiled whisk and stir until glossy.

Pour the chocolate sauce into a dessert bowl. Place 2 pear halves on top of the sauce and top with the ice cream. Serve.

Poached Pear with Rum Butter

Two poached (or canned) pear halves are baked in a bath of rum and butter. The delicacy of the pear acquires a smooth and sweet richness which makes a good complement for an uncomplicated entrée such as a filet of sole with fresh vegetable al dente.

To poach a pear, see Pear Belle Hélène (above).

2 poached pear halves
¼ cup rum
2 tablespoons butter
sour cream, optional

Preheat the oven to 350° F.

Place the pear halves cut-side up in a cake or pie pan. Pour the rum over the pears. Then place the butter in the center of each pear half.

Bake for 15 minutes, basting twice. Spoon the sauce over the pears and serve. Top with sour cream if desired.

PRUNES

Dried prunes are perhaps unfairly maligned. They are tasty and sweet, abundantly available, and easy to prepare. Dried prunes will keep for months if stored in a sealed container, and they can be reconstituted in small amounts as needed.

"Stewing" the prunes can be done without cooking them at all. Soak them overnight in water just to cover. Heat them in the morning if you want a hot breakfast fruit. Otherwise, they're fine cold. Try stewing prunes with lemon or orange pieces (rind and all) and a whole cinnamon stick. Remove the cinnamon and citrus after stewing.

Leftover stewed prunes can be stored in the refrigerator for up to a week. Keep them covered in their stewing liquid.

Puréed Prunes

If you stew a larger quantity of prunes than you can eat right away, the fruit can be pitted and puréed for use as a topping or in Prune Whip (p. 156). To make a purée, put pitted prunes through a food mill, or beat them with an electric mixer, or just mash them by hand until smooth. (They are too sticky for a blender.) If you care for a sweeter purée, add about 2 tablespoons sugar for each cup of purée. Taste it first, though. It's sweet already.

The purée can be frozen in ½-cup portions.

Prune Whip

This dessert was quite a surprise when I made it the first time. Who would have expected such a dreamy soufflé from a dish that sounds so frankly institutional? So few ingredients are combined with such ease and rise to such a towering height that any chef would be proud. Pour heavy cream over the soufflé once it settles, and you'll enjoy a truly delectable dessert.

You'll need a straight-sided baking dish of 1½–2-cup capacity. Fit the dish with a simple aluminum foil collar. To do this, tear off a length of foil long enough to fit around the dish with about an inch and a half to spare. Fold the foil lengthwise until it's about 2½ inches wide. Wrap this 2½-inch-wide length of foil around the top half of the outside of the baking dish and secure it by tying a string around the top of the dish or by taping the foil to the outside of the dish.

Grease the dish and the inside of the foil collar with butter and dust with powdered sugar. Refrigerate until needed.

½ cup puréed stewed prunes (p. 155)
1 tablespoon granulated sugar
2 egg whites
½ teaspoon cream of tartar, optional
heavy cream, optional

Preheat the oven to 350° F.

Combine the prunes with the sugar. Beat the egg whites (with the cream of tartar, if you like) until the peaks are stiff but not dry. Add the egg whites to the sweetened prune purée and fold them in gently with a rubber spatula until the two are evenly mixed.

Pour the prune mixture into the chilled soufflé dish and bake for 45–50 minutes. Remove the collar. Serve warm—plain or with cream.

Variation

Top the soufflé with Crème Anglaise (p. 171). Use the egg yolks left over from the prune whip as a thickener for the sauce.

French Bread Pudding

This is a light and delicious dessert which makes use of your whole wheat breadcrumbs. The pudding is sweetened only slightly, and when eaten warm and plain with a glass of milk, it is a good and honest dessert.

Because the pudding has a neutral, unassuming character, it is quite flexible and can be adapted to your taste. Molasses can be substituted for the sugar, for example. Stewed chopped apricots, pears, or prunes can be used in place of the raisins or currants. A fruit sauce made from heated jam or fresh berries can be spooned over the top, and of course cream would be a good choice as well.

1 egg, separated
¾ cup milk
¾ cup fine breadcrumbs (toast bread cubes in the oven, then whirl them in the blender)
1½ tablespoons brown sugar
¼ teaspoon nutmeg
1 teaspoon granulated sugar
2 tablespoons raisins or currants, plumped in warm water, optional

Preheat the oven to 350° F.

Stir the egg yolk into the milk. Add to the milk mixture the breadcrumbs, brown sugar, and nutmeg. Stir to moisten. Allow the mixture to sit while you prepare the egg white.

In a separate mixing bowl, whip the egg white into soft peaks. Add the granulated sugar and whip until the peaks are stiff but not dry. Fold the egg whites into the breadcrumb mixture, add the raisins, and pour the mixture into a greased individual pudding dish for baking.

Make a water bath by placing the pudding dish in an ovenproof pan with enough hot water to come halfway up the side of the dish. Bake for 45 minutes. The pudding is done when a sharp knife inserted into the center comes out clean. Serve when the pudding has cooled **to warm or room temperature.**

Pasta Kugel

Kugel is a traditional Jewish dish which is reminiscent of old-fashioned bread pudding. This version makes good use of leftover pasta and keeps very well. It's tasty cold, and makes a handy snack or dessert in a bag lunch.

The recipe here provides a hearty portion, and you may want to divide the kugel in half once baked. Then again, you may want to double the recipe, which is easily done.

Fettuccine is a standard choice of noodle, akin to the flat egg noodle sold in supermarkets. If you are going to use a larger pasta, chop it up before mixing.

1 egg, beaten
½ cup milk
¼ teaspoon cinnamon
½ cup cooked noodles
2–3 tablespoons raisins or currants
2 tablespoons chopped nuts

Preheat the oven to 350° F.

Combine the egg, milk, and cinnamon, and pour this mixture over the cooked noodles. Stir in the raisins and nuts. Pour the kugel into a greased baking dish and bake for 40 minutes. Cool to room temperature and serve plain or with a fruit sauce (p. 175).

Fromage Blanc

My introduction to this dish came while I was vacationing in Dijon, France. At an out-of-the-way, rough-hewn, and earthy restaurant, a patrician gentleman looking much like Charles DeGaulle sat nobly at his table eating a plain, white concoction over which he sprinkled crystals of sugar. We ordered the same. Oh, la la! Fromage Blanc avec Crème Fraîche!

In addition to a topping of Crème Fraîche, any berry sauce, particularly one made with fresh berries, would be delicious.

To proceed, you'll need a thin, clean dishcloth or cheesecloth, a colander or large strainer, and a cooking thermometer.

2 cups whole milk
4 tablespoons buttermilk
Crème Fraîche (p. 177) or berry sauce (p. 175), optional

Warm the milk to 90° F. Place it in a jar and add the buttermilk. Shake the jar to distribute the buttermilk, and then place a lid on the jar. Allow the mixture to sit at room temperature for 16 hours. When finished, the consistency will be custard-like. Don't stir it.

Pour this into a cheesecloth-lined colander and drain for 3 hours. Transfer to a clean jar and refrigerate until you're ready to serve.

Adam's American Indian Pudding

This dessert is truly an American classic. It's a mild pudding, well suited for a cold day. Part of the charm of American Indian Pudding is that it is just right when eaten plain, fresh out of the oven.

The pudding is thickened by a very small amount of cornmeal. You may use plain or polenta-grade, but either choice should be the undegermed variety. While the degermed form commonly sold in supermarkets will work, it won't have as many nutrients.

¾ cup milk
1½ tablespoons cornmeal
1 tablespoon molasses
¼ teaspoon ginger
⅛ teaspoon salt
⅛ teaspoon cinnamon
⅛ teaspoon nutmeg
1 teaspoon butter

Preheat the oven to 300° F.

Combine the milk and cornmeal in a saucepan and heat over medium heat, stirring constantly. Add the remaining ingredients and continue to stir for about 15 minutes, or until the mixture begins to thicken. Pour the mixture into a greased and floured individual casserole dish and bake for 1 hour. Serve warm or at room temperature.

Almond Cakelet

This cake is small and very rich. Try eating one serving plain and one with vanilla ice cream. The recipe calls for almond paste, but you can use marzipan if you mix it with the sugar first, then the butter. Marzipan is more cohesive and candy-like than almond paste, and you may have trouble with lumps otherwise. If you still have lumps, force the batter through a strainer and continue. What's a few lumps?

¼ cup granulated sugar
2 tablespoons butter, softened
2 ounces almond paste or marzipan
1 egg, slightly beaten
1 tablespoon kirsch
1 drop almond extract
1 tablespoon unbleached, all-purpose flour
¼ teaspoon baking powder

Preheat the oven to 350° F.

Combine the sugar, butter, and almond paste in a mixing bowl. Blend well. Add the egg, kirsch, and almond extract, and mix again. Finally, stir in the flour and the baking powder. Turn the batter into a buttered and floured individual casserole dish and bake for 25 minutes. Turn the cake onto a rack for cooling. Then serve.

Applesauce Cake

This recipe will make more than you can eat right away, but I include it because it's a fun method of cooking, the cake is very tasty, and it makes a great gift. Call up a neighbor and offer him or her half while it's still warm.

You make the applesauce first, and gradually combine the rest of the ingredients in the same saucepan. No need to dirty a bowl. If you have applesauce on hand, omit the apple, the water, and half of the sugar, then proceed.

1 medium-sized cooking apple
¾ cup water
½ cup brown sugar, packed
1 teaspoon allspice
⅓ cup raisins
¼ cup chopped nuts
1¼ cups unbleached, all-purpose flour
1 egg, slightly beaten
1 teaspoon baking soda

Preheat the oven to 350° F.

Peel, core, and dice the apple. Place it in a saucepan with a lid. Add the water and cover. Bring the water to a boil and reduce the heat to a simmer. Simmer for 6–7 minutes, until the apple is tender. Add the brown sugar, allspice, raisins, and nuts. Allow the mixture to cool for about 10 minutes.

Add ½ cup of the flour to the applesauce and stir until mixed. Add the beaten egg and the baking soda. Then add the remaining ¾ cup of flour and mix. Turn the batter into a greased and floured loaf pan and bake for 35–40 minutes, or until a knife inserted into the center of the loaf comes out clean. The cake can remain in the pan to cool; it keeps more of its moisture that way.

This recipe is one you can use for any kind of pie, be it main-dish or dessert. When successfully made, it is the texture that is a show-stopper—it's flaky and light. This is achieved by cutting a solid fat into the flour with two knives or a pastry blender, then adding just enough liquid to hold the dough together.

This recipe will provide a top and bottom crust for a single-portion pie (about 5 inches in diameter). Unbleached, all-purpose flour produces the desired light result for desserts, while whole wheat flour is a good sturdy choice for a main-dish pie.

If you don't have a rolling pin, use an empty bottle with a long, smooth body, label removed. A wine bottle is perfect for this.

1 cup unbleached, all-purpose or whole wheat flour
⅛ teaspoon salt
⅓ cup shortening, butter, or lard
4 tablespoons water, citrus juice, or milk

Combine the flour and salt in a medium-sized mixing bowl, and add the shortening.

Using a pastry blender or two knives, cut the shortening into the flour until the pieces of shortening are the size of small peas. Pour all of the liquid into the center of the flour mixture. Stir with a fork from the moist center in an outward circle until a ball begins to form. Avoid overhandling the dough.

Use your hands to complete the formation of the dough, using a **firm, gentle kneading motion. The dough should remain pliable. If the dough is quite stiff and large cracks form as you finish working the** dough, add 2 more teaspoons of water. The dough won't be as light, but it will be far more manageable.

Divide the dough in half. If you are making a single-crust dish, wrap the half you will not be using in plastic wrap and freeze it. Later

when you need it, it will take 1 hour to thaw.

To roll the dough, first sprinkle a clean breadboard with a light coat of unbleached, all-purpose flour. Form a smooth, flattened ball with the dough and place it on the breadboard. Using your hand, dust the rolling pin with flour as well.

Gently roll the dough from the center to the edge of the breadboard, repeating this motion so that the dough grows in an ever-widening circle. Press outward, rather than smashing downward. Keep checking to see that the dough doesn't stick. If it does, and it often will, free it from the board with a knife and re-flour the board. At this point you may also flip the dough and re-dust the rolling pin. If splitting occurs, roll *into* the split to "heal" it. Rolling will be complete when the dough is ⅛ inch thick *and* the edge of the dough is ¾ inch wider than the rim of the tart pan you will be using.

Place the rolled crust in the tart pan by either folding it in half (don't do this if you think it will crack) or lifting it with the aid of a broad spatula. Once the dough is in place, fold up the overlapping edges to form a thickened rim. Then crimp the edge by pinching the dough around the circle.

Your next step depends on how you intend to fill the crust. If you are going to make a tart, the pie crust should be prebaked since the tart doesn't need prolonged cooking. Prebaking should be done in a 400° F. oven, and the crust should be pricked in several places to keep it from bubbling. Baking takes about 10 minutes, but check it after 8 minutes to make sure no dark spots are developing. The crust should be cool to the touch before it is filled.

For baking a pie such as pumpkin or apple (a 2-crust pie), the dough is baked right along with the pie filling, and no pricking of the bottom crust is needed. If you have a 2-crust pie, the top crust should be pricked, however, and this is your opportunity to decorate. A fleur-de-lis, your initials, anything!

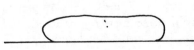

flattened ball of dough

rolling motion from center outward

rolling into crack to "heal" it

Tart Pastry

Tart pastry is a sweet pastry made with an egg instead of the water used in the standard Flaky Pastry (p. 162). The egg gives the dough the resistance to moisture which is necessary in a crust for fruit tarts. At the same time, the crust will be flaky and light— essential qualities for any pastry.

Ideally, a tart is a very flat pastry, and the sides are formed by the pastry crust to a height of only about one-half inch. Select your tart pan with this in mind, although you may have to improvise somewhat. An individual casserole dish, or ramekin, with low sides is a good choice, and metal individual pie pans also work well. Try to avoid a deep, vertical-sided container, since the crust recipe may not be adequate to cover the surface, and the crust may collapse inward as the tart bakes.

In combining the ingredients, move quickly and authoritatively, then stop. The initial mixing must be thorough for the dough to behave as it should, and if you are hesitant and tentative at this stage, the dough will have to be kneaded more later in order for it to hold together. Prolonged kneading is <u>not</u> desirable in pastry cooking, as it is in breadmaking.

This directive may seem to define a narrow margin of tolerance: On the one hand, mix the ingredients thoroughly—on the other, don't overwork the dough. Pastry is temperamental, and these words are intended to forewarn the initiate. As a novice pastry cook too young to swear, I often wept in frustration at the diabolical contrariness of mere flour and water. I do believe you can skip that stage by observing the guidelines set down here. The butter should be soft and creamy— <u>not</u> melted. Measure the salt carefully to avoid saltiness and toughness.

1 cup unbleached, all-purpose flour
1 egg, slightly beaten
¼ cup butter, softened
3 tablespoons granulated sugar
¼ teaspoon salt

Instead of mixing the ingredients in a bowl, try this technique: Make a circle of flour on a breadboard and place the remaining ingredients in the center. Mix the dough with a fork at first. Then, concentrating on keeping the consistency of the center mixture as uniform as possible, gradually incorporate the flour.

Once the center begins to thicken, start using your fingers, keeping them dusted with flour to avoid stickiness. Use a light kneading pattern of folding and pressing to incorporate all of the flour into the dough. Don't let it become stiff. It should remain pliable. The proportions given provide ample moisture, but should your dough *start* to become too firm to roll, stop kneading it and remove it from the remaining flour.

Form the dough into two balls of equal size. Wrap one ball in plastic wrap and freeze it for another time, if you wish. Place the remaining ball in the refrigerator for at least an hour before rolling out the dough.

To roll the dough, *lightly* flour a clean breadboard, and dust your rolling pin with flour as well. Form a slightly flattened ball with the dough; the sides should be perfectly smooth and free of cracks. Cracks will bring you grief, so if any appear at the very start (they will appear later and it is not such a problem), moisten your hands and gently smooth the dough's rough edges. Gently depress the dough with the rolling pin—never smash the dough—and roll away from the center in small, even strokes. The dough should grow wider and thinner in roughly concentric circles. From time to time, check under the dough to make sure it isn't sticking to the board. If it is, lift the dough with a knife or spatula, dust the board, flip the dough, dust it lightly, and resume rolling on the new side.

The dough is the correct size when it is ¾ inch wider than the perimeter of your tart pan. If it is still pliable, fold it in half and place it in the tart pan, then unfold it. If the dough is stiff, use a spatula and gingerly lift it into place without folding. Crimp the overlapping dough into a fluted edge before adding the filling.

The baking procedure you follow will be provided in the individual tart and pie recipes. As a general guideline, prebake the tart dough if the filling doesn't require long baking. Prick the dough before it goes into a 400° F. oven. Allow it to cook for about 10 minutes, checking after 8 minutes for dark spots and removing the crust from the oven if necessary. Then allow it to cool before filling.

If the filling requires or can stand prolonged cooking (more than 25 minutes), the tart crust can cook along with it. Generally, tarts are an open (as opposed to 2-crust) pie, so there is less opportunity for decorating the top crust. But if you have a top crust, you must decorate it!

Peach Tart

Fresh or canned peach wedges form spokes in the wheel of a tart shell, and are topped with a rich custard. When baked, the result is puffy and golden, and not overly sweet.

Have an uncooked tart shell ready.

1 medium-sized peach, or 8–10 slices of canned peaches
1 uncooked tart shell (p. 164)
1 tablespoon unbleached, all-purpose flour
2 tablespoons brown sugar
1 egg, slightly beaten
2 tablespoons butter, melted and slightly cooled
1 drop almond extract, optional

Preheat the oven to 350° F.

Peel and slice a peach. Arrange the peach slices in an attractive wheel in the tart shell. In a mixing bowl combine the flour, brown sugar, slightly beaten egg, butter, and almond extract. Pour this mixture over the peach slices. Bake for 30 minutes. Serve.

Tarte au Pomme

This is a great tart to make in the fall when cooking apples are at their freshest and homemade applesauce is on hand. Once baked, the tart can be glazed with a thin layer of Orange Sauce. It is pretty enough to grace any baker's window.

Have an uncooked tart shell ready.

1 uncooked tart shell (p. 164)
½ cup applesauce
1 small cooking apple, cored but unpeeled, sliced in thin wedges
1 tablespoon powdered sugar
Orange Sauce (p. 176), optional

Preheat the oven to 350° F.

Line the bottom of the tart shell with the applesauce. Arrange the apple wedges on top of the applesauce in attractive, overlapping rows, slightly immersed in the applesauce. Top with a light, even layer of powdered sugar. This is best achieved by using a sifter or other fine sieve. You might try a wire mesh tea strainer.

Bake the tart for 25 minutes. Top with Orange Sauce, if desired.

Tarte aux Abricots

We must give the French credit for this sumptuous creation. The tart is a fantasy of deep orange circles. Halved apricots are arranged over a rich apricot purée, then topped with whipped cream.

This dish is made with dried unsulphured apricots which are gently stewed first. The advantage of this is that dried apricots are available any time. There is a ready supply in the markets the year round, and once at home they keep for months. Of course, dried apricots make such good snacks that keeping them around may be a problem. Set about twenty halves aside with this recipe in mind, and your will power will be amply rewarded.

Have an uncooked tart shell ready in a suitable tart pan. Keep it refrigerated until ready to fill.

20 dried apricot halves
1½ cups water
¼ cup brown sugar
¼ cup apricot brandy, optional
1 tablespoon cornstarch
¼ cup cold water
1 uncooked tart shell (p. 164)
whipped cream, optional

Preheat the oven to 350° F.

In a small saucepan gently simmer the apricots in the water, sugar, and brandy, if desired. Stir occasionally. After about 30 minutes, remove 10 of the most attractive apricot halves to a plate. Cover the plate to prevent the apricots from drying out.

Continue to stew the remaining mixture until it is quite soft. This will take about 15 more minutes. Stir more vigorously to break up the apricot pieces as they cook. Then mash the mixture until it is smooth. Dissolve the cornstarch in the ¼ cup water. Add the dissolved cornstarch and, if necessary, a little more water to the mashed apricots. The purée shouldn't be too thick at first. It should be of pouring consistency. Continue stirring until the cornstarch is completely incorporated and the purée is glossy.

Pour the thick purée into the tart shell. Arrange the remaining 10 apricot halves attractively on top, semi-immersed in the purée. Bake for 25 minutes, then cool before serving. Top with whipped cream, if desired.

MILK CUSTARDS & PUDDINGS

Below is a summary of the many ways you can make puddings and custards with milk or cream. If you get a sudden yen for something warm, substantial, and sweet, there's a lot you can do to satisfy it—chances are you'll have the ingredients for at least one of these desserts on hand. They share a few common elements: They are dairy-based, they have both a sweetener and a thickener, and they are cooked. The characteristics of each kind of pudding or custard are summarized to help you decide which to try.

Baked Custard (p. 169) is a straightforward combination of milk and an egg, sweetened with some sugar and vanilla and baked in a water bath.

Crème Caramel (p. 169) is a baked custard with a twist: The baking dish is lined with caramelized sugar which coats the custard as it bakes. Once baked, the custard is inverted onto a dessert plate for serving.

Blanc Mange (p. 170) is a milk pudding thickened only with cornstarch, which makes it very inexpensive. The sweetness can vary greatly, depending on how much sugar you add, and many people prefer this pudding because it isn't rich. It's delicious when hot and not yet set.

Crème Anglaise (p. 171) is often used as a sauce for fruit or dessert. Like the custard, it is a combination of milk and egg (often with an extra yolk), but it is cooked on top of the stove. The thickness and sweetness can vary according to your taste. If you want it to set, add some cornstarch dissolved in cold milk.

Chocolate Pudding is an adaptation of Blanc Mange or Crème Anglaise. One or two ounces of sweet or semi-sweet chocolate are melted in a saucepan, and the milk is then added to it.

Baked Custard

An individual custard is a perfect little unit—delicate, smooth, and light. The combination of whole milk and an egg isn't rich or creamy; it's subtle, simple. Custard is easy to make, so you can enjoy it often.

1 egg, slightly beaten
2 tablespoons granulated sugar
pinch salt
¼ teaspoon vanilla
¾ cup scalded milk

Preheat the oven to 350° F.

Butter two individual custard cups of ½-cup capacity, or a single baking dish of 1-cup capacity.

In a mixing bowl, combine the egg with the sugar, salt, and vanilla. Add the scalded milk to this mixture, stirring constantly. Pour the liquid into the custard cups.

In a baking dish large enough to hold both custard cups, add 1 inch of hot water. Place the custard cups in the water. Bake for 50 minutes, or until a knife inserted into the center comes out clean. Serve.

Variation: Crème Caramel

In a heavy skillet or enamel saucepan, heat ¼ cup granulated sugar over high heat. Gently shake the pan from time to time. The sugar will melt, then become a caramel color. Pour half the caramelized sugar into one clean custard cup and swirl it around immediately to coat the bottom and sides of the dish. Repeat for the second custard cup. The liquid sugar will harden on contact with the custard cup, so move quickly. Don't worry if it coats the cup imperfectly. Fill the caramelized cups with the Baked Custard mixture and bake. Invert onto a dessert plate to serve.

Blanc Mange

How many of us stumbled over these words while reading <u>Little Women</u>? It was a shock to learn that it was mere cornstarch pudding, although I might have guessed. What else could that poor household afford to make that would be so delicious and nourishing?

The sugar in the ingredient listing is according to my own taste of a moderately sweet pudding. You may add up to 3 tablespoons if you desire. Similarly, the cornstarch produces a pudding that is creamy and not firmly set. You may add an additional table-spoon if you want a firmer result.

You'll want to make this pudding in a heavy saucepan or double boiler.

¾ cup milk
pinch salt
1 tablespoon granulated sugar
1 tablespoon cornstarch
¼ teaspoon vanilla

Heat ½ cup of the milk over medium heat with the salt and sugar. Combine the remaining ¼ cup of cold milk with the corn-starch and stir until the cornstarch is smooth. Pour the cornstarch mix-ture into the warming milk, whisk-ing it in quickly with a coiled whisk.

Continue to stir the pudding with a wooden spoon over medium to medium-low heat until it thickens. After it thickens, reduce the heat slightly and continue to cook for another 10 minutes or so. Taste the pudding to make certain there is no taste of raw cornstarch.

Remove the pudding from the burner and add the vanilla. Serve the pudding warm; or cover and refrigerate until chilled and set, and serve cold.

Crème Anglaise

This version makes a moderately rich sauce which can be eaten plain or used to top fruit or pudding. You may vary it by using half-and-half instead of milk. Also, if you want the sauce to thicken as for a pudding, dissolve 1 tablespoon cornstarch in ¼ cup of the milk and stir it into the mixture first. Once the cornstarch has had a chance to cook, then stir in the beaten egg yolks. The amount of sugar specified produces a moderately sweet result. You may double it if you choose.

Choose a heavy saucepan or double boiler to make this sauce.

1½ tablespoons granulated sugar
2 egg yolks, slightly beaten
¾ cup milk
¼ teaspoon vanilla

In a mixing bowl combine the sugar with the beaten egg yolks. In a saucepan or double boiler, scald the milk and add the hot milk to the egg mixture, whisking quickly as you pour it in. Return the mixture to the pan and cook over medium to medium-low heat, stirring constantly until it begins to thicken. Do not let it boil. Pour the sauce into a bowl and stir in the vanilla.

To chill the sauce, place the bowl in a larger bowl filled with ice and cover it to prevent a skin from forming on the surface of the pudding. Stir the mixture from time to time to allow the hot pudding in the center to reach the bowl's icy surface.

If you want to serve a warm pudding, remove it from the ice when it has reached the desired temperature. You may wish to strain the Crème Anglaise through a wire mesh strainer at this stage, but if there are no lumps, the step is unnecessary.

SAUCES

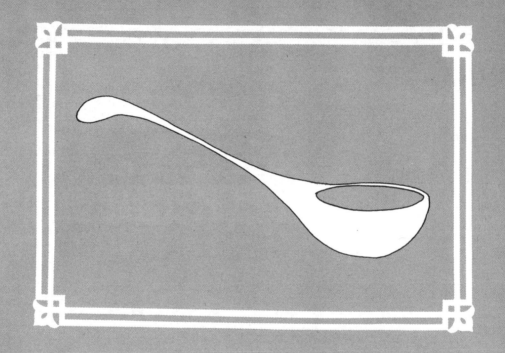

The French have taught us a great deal about the value of sauces. A simple sauce, made from the most elementary of ingredients, can turn even a humdrum dish into something special and sophisticated. A savory gravy can be put together in just a few minutes to dress up a meat entrée. A tangy cheese sauce adds a terrific contrast to vegetables and casseroles—just pick your cheese! And desserts can be taken from the excellent to the sublime with the addition of a sauce. A sauce is the perfect finishing touch for almost any culinary creation.

FRUIT SAUCES

The tasty fruit sauce comes from many quarters: The jam pot, the juice pitcher, and fresh berries are the most noteworthy. Regardless of the source, the fruit sauce will enhance almost any pudding, cake, or custard.

One does not go out and shop for the ingredients in a fruit sauce. One looks at the materials at hand and uses them creatively. Recently I was in a country cabin away from any store, and I had made French Bread Pudding (p. 157). For a fruit sauce, I combined the tail end of the Thanksgiving cranberry sauce with the last of the orange juice. I had to stretch the sauce with water, but by adding lemon juice and sugar I was able to adjust the taste, and it was just fine. The only thickener I had was flour, but I allowed plenty of time for the sauce to cook, so there was no starchy taste. I've really told you all you need to know, but have nevertheless provided additional ideas in recipe form.

Basic berry sauce. For each cup of berries, mashed after measuring, add 1–2 tablespoons sugar (to taste) and 1–2 teaspoons lemon juice (to taste). Dissolve ½ teaspoon cornstarch in 2 tablespoons water and add to the berry mixture. Heat, stirring constantly, until the sauce becomes shiny and loses its starchy taste.

Stir in 1 tablespoon of liqueur if desired (triple sec, Grand Marnier, kirsch, for example). Pour the sauce over ice cream or pudding.

Chilled fruit sauce. In a blender place 1 pear, peeled and cubed; 2 ice cubes; 2 fresh mint leaves; 1 teaspoon lemon juice; and 3 tablespoons vermouth or pear liqueur. Blend until smooth. Pour over chilled melon or strawberry halves.

Jam sauce. Melt 2 teaspoons butter in a 5-inch skillet or small saucepan. Add 3–4 tablespoons jam and heat through. Thin with lemon juice or fruit juice if necessary. Use as a topping for dessert crêpes (p. 49).

Lemon Sauce

⅓ CUP

This sauce is delicious over Brown Betty (p. 152) and French Bread Pudding (p. 157)—among other things.

2 teaspoons cornstarch
1 tablespoon cold water
2 tablespoons lemon juice (juice of 1 lemon)
4 tablespoons granulated sugar
1 teaspoon grated lemon peel

Dissolve the cornstarch in the cold water. Then combine all the ingredients and heat until the cloudiness disappears and the sauce is a shiny yellow.

Orange Sauce

⅓ CUP

Particularly scrumptious as a topping for Tarte au Pomme (p. 166), this fruit sauce can be whipped up in no time.

2 teaspoons granulated sugar
⅓ cup orange juice
2 teaspoons cornstarch
2 teaspoons cold water

In a small saucepan over low heat, dissolve the sugar in the orange juice. Then dissolve the cornstarch in the water. Turn up the heat to medium. Add the cornstarch mixture to the pan and stir constantly until the mixture is clear and free of any cornstarch taste—about 6 minutes. Remove the sauce from the burner and spoon it over your dessert. Cool slightly before serving.

Crème Fraîche

This version is very close to the real thing; the French use raw milk, while we substitute half-and-half. The result will be creamy and thick—an elegant topping. The recipe for its classic companion, Fromage Blanc, can be found on p. 159.

1 cup half-and-half
1 teaspoon buttermilk

Combine the ingredients and heat the mixture to 85° F. Use a cooking thermometer to test the temperature. Remove the thermometer, place the mixture in a jar with a lid, and set it on top of your stove. Don't put the jar over the pilot light. Leave it until it has thickened, usually about 15 hours. Stir gently, then refrigerate. Crème Fraîche can be kept for several weeks.

Basic White Sauce

Basic may be an understatement for this sauce. It can be used for almost anything, and its character is easily altered by the addition of spices or other flavorings. See the Basic Cheese Sauce, below, for one simple variation.

2 teaspoons butter
2 teaspoons unbleached, all-purpose
  flour
¾ cup milk
pinch salt
pinch pepper

Melt the butter over medium heat. Then add the flour and stir. Cook for about 30 seconds. Gradually add the milk, stirring constantly and briskly with a wire whisk to prevent lumps. Season to taste with salt and pepper. Cook for about 5 minutes. The sauce should be of medium thickness.

Basic Cheese Sauce

This rather routine recipe can open many doors. The wide variety of cheeses available suggests myriad variations. Cheese sauces can completely change the character of foods, and they can dress up leftovers like nothing else. Consider a Gruyère sauce over the Mushroom Timbale (p. 93) or Broccoli Frittata (p. 15).

2 teaspoons butter
2 teaspoons unbleached, all-purpose
  flour
¾ cup milk
⅓ cup grated brick-type cheese (such
  as cheddar or Jack)
⅛ teaspoon dry mustard, optional

Melt the butter in a sauté pan and add the flour to it. Gradually add the milk, and cook for about 3 minutes, stirring constantly to keep the sauce from lumping. The sauce will thicken. Add the cheese and mustard and stir over low heat until the cheese is melted and evenly distributed throughout the sauce. Serve.

Hollandaise Sauce

This recipe makes two portions since it can't be further divided successfully. Use the other half within two days. It can be used as a topping for a baked or mashed potato, steamed vegetables, chilled fish, sliced tomato, a frittata, or broiled meat.

2 egg yolks
1 tablespoon lemon juice
dash salt
⅓ cup butter

Place everything but the butter into a blender jar and whirl for 5 seconds.

Melt the butter to the bubbly stage. Then turn the blender on again and pour the hot butter into the blender slowly, in a thin stream. Take about 20 seconds to pour in the butter. When you have finished pouring, the sauce is ready to serve.

You can keep the sauce warm by putting the blender jar in a bowl of hot water.

Pesto Sauce

1 CUP

This is the way to eat basil, particularly if you can eat it with fresh pasta (although I have a friend who eats it on bagels!). This recipe is designed to use a standard bunch of fresh basil. You will probably want to freeze a portion of the sauce, so note that not all of the ingredients are added before freezing. The Parmesan cheese and the pine nuts are added after the sauce has thawed, because the pesto doesn't taste nearly as fresh if the pine nuts and Parmesan aren't just added.

2 cups loosely packed fresh basil leaves
2 medium-sized garlic cloves, chopped
1 teaspoon salt
¾ cup olive oil
¼ cup pine nuts (pignolia)
2 tablespoons grated Parmesan cheese

If you're not going to freeze any of the sauce, combine all the ingredients in a blender, and blend until the mixture is smooth. Then serve or refrigerate until needed.

If you are going to freeze some or all of the sauce, blend only the first four ingredients and put the amount to be frozen into containers holding ¼- to ⅓-cup portions. To complete the sauce, defrost a frozen portion and place it in a blender with 1 tablespoon pine nuts and 2 teaspoons grated Parmesan cheese. Blend until smooth. Serve.

178   COOKING FOR SOMEONE SPECIAL—YOURSELF

Yogurt

Making yogurt involves the introduction of a yogurt culture into milk, then stabilizing the temperature to permit the culture to grow. Much of what is written on yogurt technique has to do with temperature control. You will need a cooking thermometer unless you have an electric yogurt maker. My own preference is to make the yogurt in a large thermos which has been warmed to about 110° F. To achieve this, add hot water to the thermos and adjust the temperature to 110° F. using a thermometer to test. Seal the thermos until it is needed, then quickly pour out the water and substitute the milk mixture, which has been heated to the same temperature. Once the thermos is sealed, the yogurt can be cultured free from drafts or risk of overheating.

If the pilot temperature is adequate and stable, you may place the culturing yogurt in your oven.

2 cups milk

1 tablespoon plus 1 teaspoon plain yogurt

Scald the milk, and allow it to cool to 110° F. Add the plain yogurt. The yogurt can be taken from a container you have on hand if it's fresh. Mix thoroughly. Place the mixture in a thermos or another environment at 110° F. for 4 hours. Remove to a clean jar with a lid, and refrigerate until needed.

⋟ LABNI ⋞

From the Middle East comes this soft and somewhat tart cheese which is *the* alternative to high-fat cheeses. It is made with low-fat yogurt! Also, it keeps for two or three weeks when refrigerated.

The yogurt does all but about 1 minute of the work. Form a bag from a square of cheesecloth and place the yogurt inside. Hang this from your kitchen or bathroom faucet overnight. Then season the yogurt with your choice of chives, paprika, salt, onion, dill weed, or parsley. Refrigerate in a covered container.

If you enjoy breakfast cheeses, you'll like this on a piece of dry or buttered toast. Sweeten it with honey to taste, if you like. For lunch or snacking it is quite tasty when spread on crackers or wholesome bread along with tomato or cucumber slices.

Vegetable Marinade

½ CUP

There is so much leeway in making a marinade that it seems a shame to show just one recipe. Don't hesitate to vary the ratio of oil to vinegar if you want a lighter result. The dill weed and thyme can be omitted and substituted with the fresh or dried herb of your own choosing.

⅜ cup vegetable oil
⅛ cup vinegar
pinch salt
pinch pepper
⅛ teaspoon dill weed
1 tablespoon chopped parsley
⅛ teaspoon thyme
1 garlic clove, sliced

Combine all the ingredients. Pour over vegetables and allow them to marinate in the refrigerator for up to 24 hours before serving.

Peanut Butter Dressing

⅓ CUP

This dressing is a little unusual, but note that its ingredients are easily acquired and probably on hand. It is very tasty and takes very little time to make. It offers distinction to the Peanut Rice Salad (p. 74) and is also a real standout as a dressing for fresh spinach leaves. The role it can play in leftover vegetables also can be quite creative. Chilled carrots, cooked and sliced, are a very tasty companion to Peanut Butter Dressing.

1 teaspoon vegetable oil
1 tablespoon minced onion
1 small garlic clove, crushed
½ teaspoon grated fresh ginger
2 tablespoons water
1 tablespoon peanut butter (chunky or smooth)
2 tablespoons milk
2 teaspoons lemon juice
1 teaspoon honey, optional

Heat the oil in a small frying pan, and lightly brown the onion, garlic, and ginger in the hot oil. Add the water and peanut butter and stir until the peanut butter is blended in. Add the milk and stir again. Finally, stir in the lemon juice (and honey, if desired), turn off the heat, and serve when cooled.

Cashew Sauce

This cashew sauce is creamy and light, well suited to all sorts of steamed vegetables.

2 teaspoons butter
2 teaspoons unbleached, all-purpose flour
⅓ cup half-and-half
⅓ cup chicken broth or water
⅓ cup cashews, chopped (they can be chopped in a blender)
⅛ teaspoon celery salt
½ teaspoon Worcestershire sauce

Melt the butter in a sauté pan. Add the flour and stir for 60 seconds. Gradually add the half-and-half, continuing to stir to avoid lumps. Add the broth, stir to mix, and then add the remaining ingredients. Pour the hot sauce over steamed vegetables and serve.

Vegetable Pasta Sauce

This sauce has rich substance and flavor. The vegetables are cooked only briefly, for the al dente consistency is what makes the sauce a success. If you don't have spinach on hand, omit it. In fact, use a free hand with the vegetables you do have. Select fettuccine or an even wider noodle, as the sauce coats the pasta quite nicely.

2 tablespoons olive oil
1 garlic clove, sliced
½ eggplant, diced
½ zucchini, cut in ½-inch discs
2 medium-sized tomatoes, diced
½ teaspoon basil or oregano
¼ teaspoon fennel seed, crushed
⅛ teaspoon salt
pinch pepper
1 4-ounce can tomato sauce
⅓ cup chopped spinach leaves, optional
¾–1 cup cooked pasta
2 tablespoons grated Parmesan cheese

Heat the oil, add the garlic to it, and stir. After 15–20 seconds, add the eggplant and zucchini and sauté for about 2 minutes, stirring constantly. Add the diced tomatoes, the spices, and the salt and pepper, stir briefly, then add the tomato sauce and spinach and cover. Reduce the heat and simmer for 10–12 minutes. Toss the pasta with grated Parmesan cheese, pour the sauce over it and serve.

Béchamel Sauce

Béchamel Sauce revives leftover casseroles with great success. It is the suggested topping for the Mushroom Timbale (p. 93), and it would be excellent as a topping for leftover frittata or an extra fish filet. Also, Béchamel Sauce is the sauce used in Egg Florentine (p. 10).

The technique used in making Béchamel Sauce is the same used for a wide number of white sauces. After you've made it about a dozen times, you'll realize that there's a trend here: You melt the butter, you add the flour and let it cook, you add the milk and let it thicken. The rest is just a variation on this theme, and there are many variations. Grate cheese into the milk and you've got a cheese sauce. Sprinkle a little curry powder in and you've got an Indian cream sauce. I hope you will get to know this sauce, then the technique, and begin to improvise.

Store any unused sauce in the refrigerator for up to two days.

2 teaspoons butter
½ teaspoon onion (approximately)
1 tablespoon unbleached, all-purpose flour
1 cup milk
pinch salt
pinch white pepper
pinch nutmeg

In a small frying pan, melt the butter. Grate the onion very fine directly into the melting butter. (You may want to measure the first few times.) Let the onion heat through. Add the flour to the butter and mix it well. Reduce the heat and cook this roux until it is slightly browned, about 2 minutes.

Gradually add the milk, stirring briskly and thoroughly with a wire whisk to prevent lumping.

Season with a hint of salt. Add pepper and nutmeg. Allow the sauce to cook for 7–10 minutes over low heat. The classic Béchamel Sauce is strained before serving, but you may skip this step.

Variation: Sauce Mornay

Once the Béchamel Sauce is cooked, add 1 teaspoon grated Parmesan cheese, and stir to mix.

Marinara Seafood Sauce

This sauce can be made with only the simplest group of ingredients: garlic, fresh tomatoes, onions, salt, and pepper; it can be made more elaborate with the addition of green pepper, olives, and your choice of Italian herbs; or it can stretch all the way to becoming a bouillabaise containing fish pieces, calamari, and any shellfish you can buy. It's a classic with spaghetti.

Fresh herbs are desirable here, and Italian herbs such as fresh basil, parsley, oregano, and thyme come to mind. ♠

½ stick butter
1–2 garlic cloves, sliced
1 onion, sliced very thin
5–6 medium-sized tomatoes, sectioned
½–¾ cup red wine, water, or tomato sauce
herbs of your choice
pepper

Melt the butter in a pot. Once the butter is melted, add the garlic and onion. Sauté until the onion is translucent, then add the tomatoes and the wine.

Once the tomatoes are simmering, finely chop the fresh herbs, or crush the dried herbs, and add them to the sauce, along with fresh pepper, all according to your taste.

Allow the marinara sauce to simmer until the tomatoes are done, about 10 minutes.

Sauce Diablo

This sauce is excellent with chicken, lamb, and even steak! Its basis is the precious pan juices that remain when meat or poultry has been fried, broiled, or roasted. ♠

¼ cup chicken broth
2 tablespoons sherry or white wine
2 teaspoons Dijon, German, or English mustard
¼ cup half-and-half

Drain the pan after removing the sautéed meat. Add the broth, sherry, and mustard. Over medium heat, deglaze the pan as the mixture bubbles. Reduce the liquid slightly. Add the half-and-half and continue to reduce. Don't be afraid to let the sauce bubble as long as you continue to stir it. It should be adequately thickened in about 3 minutes. Pour over the meat and serve.

Poached Fish Sauce

Once you've made a court bouillon and poached a filet of fish, you have something too good to pass up. The court bouillon becomes the basis for a fish sauce. Unfortunately, you can't use all of it unless you want a quart of sauce. I don't recommend refrigerating or freezing court bouillon (or this sauce) because it is so fragile. Therefore, discard all but ⅓ cup of the liquid.

You can't really reduce court bouillon because it doesn't have body, so you'll have to thicken it to make a sauce.

2 teaspoons cornstarch
¼ cup white wine or vermouth
⅓ cup court bouillon (see
  Poached Red Snapper, p. 132)
1 teaspoon caviar, optional

Dissolve the cornstarch in 1 tablespoon of the wine to make a lump-free paste. Add the remaining wine to the court bouillon. Add the cornstarch paste, whisking constantly to quickly dissolve it in the court bouillon. Cook the sauce, stirring constantly over high heat, until it is thick and clear. Add the caviar and stir to mix. Heat through. Pour the sauce over fish and serve.

Savory Lemon and Cream Sauce

This sauce goes well with any lighter meat. Try it with veal as well as chicken and fish. You can make it any time you're lucky enough to have pan juices from broiled, roasted, or fried meat.

1 big squeeze lemon juice
⅓ cup whipping cream

Squeeze the lemon juice directly into the hot frying pan once the meat has been removed. Use a fork to scrape up all the flavored particles from the pan surface. This should take only a few seconds. Then add the cream and stir it. Once it bubbles vigorously, add the meat and gently coat it with the sauce. Then serve and enjoy!

Brown Gravy

Any meat that is fried or roasted leaves a part of itself behind in the pan. Those fats and juices are the basis for gravy. Short ribs, pan-fried steak, a roasted lamb shank, and hamburger patties are all generous in their contributions to this effort. The makings for gravy aren't limited to red meat—fried chicken also makes really good gravy. Remember that the gravy is made right in the pan with the pan drippings. As you add the various ingredients, keep working the meat particles free from the bottom of the pan. As they dissolve, your gravy becomes richer and richer.

To make the best use of pan juices, you may want to make a large batch of gravy and freeze it in ½-cup portions. Remember that equal parts flour and fat is the rule. Always dissolve additional thickener in cold water first, and always add liquids to the gravy slowly, stirring constantly. Use cooking liquids when available, since the vitamins in them enrich the gravy.

1½ teaspoons pan juices
1½ teaspoons unbleached, all-
  purpose flour
1 cup water or broth
salt or soy sauce
Worcestershire sauce, optional

To begin, spoon out or pour off all but 1½ teaspoons of the fat in the pan. Place the gravy pan on a burner over medium heat and sprinkle 1½ teaspoons of unbleached, all-purpose flour over the pan drippings. Stir the flour into the fat and juices in the pan. It will quickly thicken into a paste. Allow this mixture to cook for 2 minutes, stirring constantly.

Once the flour has cooked for 2 minutes, *very* slowly add 1 cup water or broth in ¼-cup increments, stirring constantly and completely, and repeating until the whole cup is added.

Reduce the heat to a simmer. Taste the gravy. Add salt or soy sauce to taste, but use it sparingly. You can also try adding Worcestershire sauce.

To thicken. Dissolve 1 teaspoon flour with 2 tablespoons cold water. Stir until smooth. Gradually add this mixture to the gravy, stirring constantly. Cook for 5 minutes or until the starchy taste is gone.

To thin. Gradually add broth or water 1 tablespoon at a time, stirring constantly.

Variation: Chicken Gravy

Remove the chicken and any vegetables to a platter and thicken the pan juices with a paste made from 2 teaspoons each of flour and cold water. Cook for about 2 minutes; then slowly stir in 1 cup water or chicken broth. Increase the heat to permit cooking for about 6 minutes, and add a teaspoon of butter, which will finish the gravy. Stir, season, and serve. If you have some chopped gizzard and heart on hand, a few tablespoons will make a nice addition to the gravy.

HERB
&
SPICE BLENDS

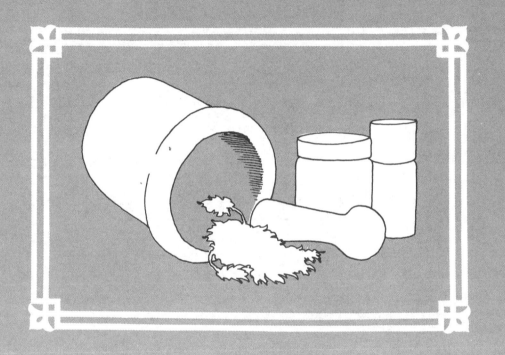

Over the past couple of thousand years people have often experimented with ways to enhance their food. In this quest for new tastes they have chipped at tree bark, ground roots, crushed seeds, torn leaves, plucked flowers, and dried pods in the sun. Some of these projects killed the would-be gourmands, some proved pointless, and some became the basis for the transformation of a culture's diet into a rich cuisine.

These days herbs and spices serve to make dull food interesting, and interesting food fascinating. While many Americans have access to a wide variety of foods, probably no more than a few dozen different types are eaten frequently by any one person. Over the years this repetition can get a little dull. Herbs and spices add variety to these foods, and at the same time they serve to challenge, stimulate, and educate the palate.

The following recipes are not only fun to make and use, they are time-tested and prized concoctions which will make a meal very special. Many of them also make lovely gifts.

Bouquet Garni

A bouquet garni is a packet of herbs and aromatic vegetables which is added to a dish as it cooks, and is removed at the end of the preparation. In this way no undesirable residue is left to mar the texture of the dish.

The components of the bouquet may vary, but usually include the ingredients listed here.

2 sprigs fresh parsley
⅛ teaspoon dried thyme leaves, crushed
½–1 bay leaf
2–3 carrot matchsticks, optional
3–4 cloves, optional (used with ragout sauces or stewing meats)
⅛ teaspoon dried marjoram leaves, crushed, optional
4 widely curving pieces of celery, about 6 inches long

Combine all the ingredients, except the celery, inside the curve of 1 celery rib and place the other ribs of celery over the first to cover the ingredients inside. Secure very tightly with white cotton string. (You may enclose the ingredients in cheesecloth instead, if you wish.) Immerse the bundle in the simmering liquid during the last hour of cooking, and remove before serving.

Battuto, or Matignon

Battuto is a paste made by finely mincing aromatic vegetables and herbs with a small amount of lean salt pork. It is used frequently in Italy and France in the preparation of red meats and heavy sauces. In cooking just for yourself, you'll want to try this paste in stews and soups where your effort will bring a greater return. The battuto is made just before it is to be used. It forms a flavor base to which other ingredients are added.

1 strip lean salt pork (a little wider than a strip of bacon and not quite as long)
¼ carrot, sliced
⅛ medium-sized onion, peeled and cut in wedges
¼ rib celery, sliced
1 medium-sized garlic clove, peeled
½ teaspoon dried rosemary, or ¼ teaspoon fresh
1 tablespoon coarsely chopped fresh parsley

On the strip of salt pork, place the remaining ingredients. With a very sharp knife, mince the vegetables by cutting through them into the salt pork. Continue cutting until you have made a paste. Brown this mixture in the bottom of your soup or stew pot.

Curry Powder

A curry powder recipe is rarely found in Middle Eastern or Indian cookbooks. Curry powder is a western method of approximating the flavors produced in eastern cooking. In that type of cuisine the various aromatics are added at different stages in food preparation and in different combinations, depending on the character of the main ingredients.

This recipe makes between ¼ and ⅓ cup of curry powder. All of these spices should be ground.

1¼ teaspoons cumin
2 teaspoons turmeric
2 teaspoons coriander
1 teaspoon ginger
½ teaspoon fenugreek
½ teaspoon cardamom
1 teaspoon dry mustard
1 teaspoon allspice
pinch cayenne
1 teaspoon cinnamon

Combine all of the ingredients and mix thoroughly. Store the mixture in a jar with a tight-fitting lid.

Fines Herbes

This classic French herb blend, useful for dressing up all manner of green salads and vegetables, is often found in clever little containers in chic little food shops. Mix your own and save! All of these herbs should be dried and crushed.

parsley
chives
tarragon
chervil
savory, optional

Combine equal parts of all the ingredients and store the mixture in a jar with a tight-fitting lid.

Garam Masala

This is a thoroughly enjoyable "warm blend" of spices added to many Indian dishes. It is not a curry. It does not sustain long cooking, so it should be added at the last minute to egg, rice, chicken, and fish dishes. Use ground spices.

1 tablespoon cardamom
2 teaspoons cinnamon
2 tablespoons coriander
1 teaspoon cloves
1½ tablespoons cumin
2 teaspoons pepper
1 teaspoon mace

Combine all of the ingredients and mix thoroughly. Store the mixture in a jar with a tight-fitting lid.

Prepared Mustard

Try making your own mustard and see how favorably it compares with what you buy at the supermarket.

1 tablespoon dry mustard or well-crushed mustard seed
2 teaspoons beer, white wine, or vinegar

Combine the ingredients and mix thoroughly. Add more liquid as needed for the desired consistency. Refrigerate in a sealed jar. When stored this way, prepared mustard will keep for several months.

Parisian Spice

There are several widely varying recipes for Parisian Spice, but this one is the tastiest when added to sautéed chicken, which is a very popular use.

Use ground spices and crushed dried herbs.

1 teaspoon basil
1 teaspoon cloves
1 teaspoon mace
1 teaspoon pepper
1 teaspoon rosemary
1 teaspoon thyme
1 bay leaf
1½ teaspoons cinnamon
pinch cayenne

Combine all of the ingredients in a blender or spice grinder. Store the mixture in a jar with a tight-fitting lid.

Savory Salt

This concoction gives nice body to cream soups, stews, and vegetables.

3 tablespoons celery salt
3 tablespoons garlic salt
3 tablespoons onion salt
1½ teaspoons paprika
1½ teaspoons chili powder
½ teaspoon pepper
¼ teaspoon cayenne

Blend all of the ingredients thoroughly and store the mixture in a spice jar with a "shaker" top in addition to its tight-fitting lid.

Quatre Épices

This mixture is literally translated "four spices"; it is a mixture of the four ground "cake spices." Quatre épices is good as a topping for French toast, or as a quick method of seasoning biscuits and custards.

1 teaspoon cloves
1 teaspoon nutmeg
1 teaspoon ginger
1 tablespoon cinnamon

Combine all of the ingredients and mix thoroughly. Store the mixture in a jar with a tight-fitting lid.

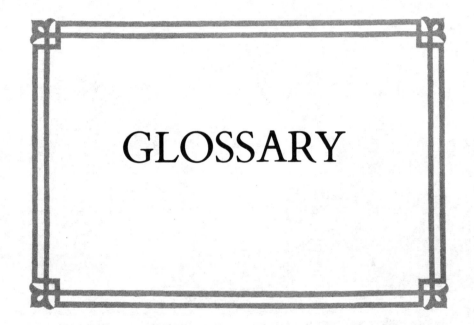

GLOSSARY

This list includes words and phrases that appear in this cookbook which may be new to you. The pronunciation guides, where provided, are intended to give you a *general* sense of the word's pronunciation; they do not represent the special nuances characteristic of each language.

Al dente *(all den' tay)*. Food that is not overcooked, but instead is still resistant to the bite. Usually refers to pasta and vegetables.

Al funghi *(all foon' gee)*. A phrase often used in the title of a dish to indicate that it features mushrooms.

Al fresco *(all fress' ko)*. Outdoors, as in dining al fresco.

Blanching. Immersing food in boiling water for anywhere from 30 seconds to 3 minutes, depending on the food type. For vegetables and fruits, blanching is a pre-freezing step. For some meats, it is a pre-cooking step. When meat is blanched it turns white, which in French is *blanche*—thus the origin of the term. The process is similar to parboiling.

Bouillon *(bool' yon)*. A seasoned broth served as a clear soup. Since all broth should be seasoned to taste as part of its preparation, bouillon and broth are usually synonymous.

Braise. The process of cooking (usually tougher) cuts of meat semi-immersed in a flavorful liquid such as broth or wine (water can also be used). Braising takes an hour or more depending on the size and cut of the meat, and can be done on stovetop or in the oven using medium-low heat.

Burrito *(boo ree' to)*. A Mexican rolled "sandwich" made with a flour tortilla and filled with beans, rice, meat, salsa, cheese, or a combination of these.

Caper. The closed bud of the flower of the caper bush which is indigenous to the Mediterranean. Capers are packed in a pickling brine which allows them to be kept, in the refrigerator, almost indefinitely once opened. Capers are used sparingly in salads and sauces to lend piquancy and textural interest to savory dishes and sauces. Menu items including "picatta" in the title generally contain capers.

Caramelize. To cook sugar until it turns a golden or deep brown color. Vegetables and meat juices that have been browned specifically to provide color and flavor to a sauce leave a dark residue on the pan surface which is also described as "caramelized."

Chèvre *(shev)*. The generic designation for French goat cheese.

Clarify. To make a cloudy liquid clear using various techniques. Butter is clarified through heating and skimming the foam and residue off the top. Soup stock is clarified through the addition of lightly whipped egg whites, which collect the clouding debris as they cook and are then removed and discarded.

Cream of tartar. A white crystalline powder sometimes added to egg whites as a stabilizing agent to assure that the whites don't separate and get watery during whipping.

Crudité *(croo' di tay')*. A cold plate of raw, marinated, and cooked vegetables sometimes served before a meal as an appetizer. It is akin to antipasto, but usually not as heavy.

Curry. A generic term used to describe a wide range of spice combinations used in Middle Eastern cooking. Curries often contain turmeric, cumin, and coriander as basic ingredients.

Defatted or degermed. Refers to the removal of the portion of the grain kernel, the germ, that contains fat and can therefore cause spoilage. Removal of the germ results in reduced nutritional value. The whole grain (undefatted) can be stored in a cool, dark place to diminish the possibility of spoilage.

Deglaze. The process of recovering caramelized pieces of vegetable or meat juices from a cooking surface by adding liquid to the pan over heat, then stirring and scraping to dissolve the morsels in the liquid.

Dollop. About a spoonful of a thickened liquid such as mayonnaise, whipped cream, or puréed vegetable or fruit used as a garnish.

Dredge. To coat (food) with a powder, such as flour or powdered sugar.

Filet (*fill ay'*). Fish that has had the bones removed. Also the process of removing bones from fish or meat.

Florentine. Refers to a dish that features spinach.

Florets or flowerettes. Cut sections of broccoli or cauliflower that take advantage of the natural branching of the vegetable. Each piece contains both "flower" and stem.

Fold. To carefully incorporate beaten egg whites or whipped cream into a thicker mixture in a way that preserves the airiness. Folding is a gentle motion, often done with a rubber spatula, consisting of cutting down into the mixture at the side of the bowl, then cutting back up through the center.

Frittata (*fri ta' ta*). A generic term for a wide range of custard-based vegetable or meat dishes that are either baked or cooked on stovetop. A frittata can be described as a crustless quiche, but it usually contains larger chunks of vegetable, seafood, or meat.

Fromage (*fro mahj'*). The French word for cheese.

Giblets. The edible organs of poultry: liver, heart, and gizzard.

Gnocchi (*nyo' key*). A small dumpling made of farina, potato, flour, or ricotta cheese and bound with egg.

Groats. Grain that has had the hull removed in milling.

Half-and-half. A mixture of equal parts of milk and cream, available commercially from most dairy companies.

Jalapeño (*hall a pain' yo*). A small, green, hot pepper popular in Mexican cooking.

Julienne. To cut (vegetables, such as potatoes and carrots, or cooked meat) into long, thin strips.

Kirsch (*keersh*). A colorless liqueur distilled from cherries.

Legume (*leg' yoom*). Beans, such as kidney beans, pinto beans, and string beans. Also peanuts.

Leavening. Ingredients added to baked goods that cause them to rise. Yeast, baking soda, and baking powder are the most common leavening agents.

Marinade. A liquid in which meats and vegetables are soaked (marinated) to increase their flavor. A marinade usually has an acid (lemon juice or wine, for example) and an oil component, in addition to herbs, spices, and perhaps some sweetener.

Parboil. To cook partially by boiling for a brief period.

Poach. To cook food in a simmering water bath which often has been flavored with spices and other like ingredients.

Proofing yeast. Mixing the yeast with water and letting it sit for five minutes gives it the head start it needs to raise the dough. At the same time, the baker can verify that the yeast is alive and well. The sign of a successfully proofed yeast mixture is the formation of tiny bubbles on the surface of the liquid.

Ramekin. An individual baking and serving dish.

Reduce. To heat a sauce or stock with the purpose of cooking away the water to produce a thicker, more concentrated and flavorful result.

Rib, celery. A whole piece, from base to leaf, of a celery stalk. A rib is sometimes referred to as a stalk; however, in this cookbook the stalk includes the ribs.

Ricotta (*ri coh' tah*). A soft, fresh cheese used in cooking. Ricotta is often added to lasagna. It is also used to stuff cannoli and manicotti, and makes a good addition to main-dish custards.

Roux (*roo*). A cooked flour and oil paste which is the lump-free means of thickening sauces and successfully cooking flour.

Salsa. "Salsa" is the Spanish word for sauce, and it is used in this book and elsewhere to refer to a Mexican sauce made primarily from tomatoes and peppers. You can buy "mild" salsa or "hot" salsa where Mexican food is sold.

Sauté (*so tay'*). To fry food in butter or oil over high heat in a pan with sloped sides in order to permit the escape of steam and the easy manipulation of the food.

Scald. To heat (a liquid) almost to the boiling point.

Scaloppine (*skal o pee' nee*). Meat or poultry that has been sliced or pounded into a thin layer, then sautéed.

Shock. To dunk cooking vegetables into cold water to stop the cooking and preserve the color.

Simmer. To heat a liquid so that it does not boil, but maintains a temperature just under boiling.

Skim. To remove unwanted material from the surface of a simmering liquid. Stock and clarified butter are skimmed in preparation.

Soufflé (*soo flay'*). A tall, light, and airy dish made by incorporating beaten egg whites into a flavorful, thicker mixture, and baking.

Stalk, celery. The portion of the celery plant that grows above the ground and consists of several ribs attached to the base of the plant.

Stock. The liquid derived from prolonged simmering of meat or vegetables in water.

Timbale (*tim' bal*). A casserole featuring vegetables, fish, or meat which may be finely chopped or puréed before baking. The timbale is baked in a vertical-sided casserole dish and is often served with a sauce.

Wheat germ. The oil-rich section of a wheat grain where the growth occurs. It is highly nutritious and contains vitamin E, which means that it must be refrigerated to avoid rancidity. It can be added to cereals, casseroles, salads, and baked goods.

Whisk. To whip or stir liquids for the purpose of mixing them and/or incorporating air, using a utensil called a whisk.

Whole grain. Refers to grain products made with wheat that has been milled to retain the bran, endosperm, and germ, rather than with refined grain which has the bran and germ removed.

Wilt. To place vegetable greens in a hot pan thinly coated with oil until the greens become limp but not soggy.

INDEX